OBJECTIVES OF SOIL SCIENCE

ICARs, JRF, SRF, ARS, NET
Indian Agricultural Research Institute-Ph.D.
Entrance Exam, State Department Exams

OBJECTIVES OF SOIL SCIENCE

ICARs, JRF, SRF, ARS, NET
Indian Agricultural Research Institute-Ph.D. Entrance Exam, State Department Exams

By

Dr. Jitendra Singh
Assistant Professor
Teerthankar Mahaveer University
Moradabad, (U.P.)
(India)

&

Dr. Robin Kumar
Research Associate
Indian Institute of Farming Systems Research
Meerut (U.P.)
(India)

DPH

DISCOVERY PUBLISHING HOUSE PVT. LTD.
INDIA

Published by:
Namit Wasan
DISCOVERY PUBLISHING HOUSE PVT. LTD.
4383/4B, Ansari Road, Darya Ganj
New Delhi-110 002 (India)
Phone : +91-11-23279245; 23253475; 43596065
E-mail : discoverybooksindia@gmail.com
discoverypublishinghouse@gmail.com
namitwasan9@gmail.com
web : www.discoverypublishinggroup.com

First Edition: **2019**

ISBN: 978-93-86841-81-0

Objectives of Soil Science

Printed at:
Infinity Imaging Systems
Delhi

Preface

This book is a compilation of objective type questions covering most of the aspects of soil science for all the competitive soil science examinations. The book will be useful for preparing competitive exams like ICARs Junior Research Fellowship (JRF), Senior Research Fellow (SRF), Agricultural Research Services (ARS), National Eligibility Test (NET), Indian Agricultural Research Institute-Ph.D., Entrance Exam, State Department Exams, etc.

Due care has been taken to omit errors and repetition but any such error brought to our notice will surely help to update the book for its subsequent editions.

–Authors

Preface

This book is a compilation of objective type questions covering most of the aspects of all subjects of the agricultural/allied sciences academics. The book will be useful in preparing competitive examinations like ICAR's Junior Research Fellowship (JRF), Senior Research Fellowship (SRF), Agricultural Research Service (ARS), National Eligibility Test (NET), Indian Agricultural Research Institute Ph.D. Entrance Exam, State Department Exams, etc.

Due care has been taken to avoid errors and suggestions in any respect brought to our notice will surely help to update the book in its subsequent editions.

Authors

Contents

CHAPTER - 1

Introductory Chemistry

1. Solution whose strength or concentration is accurately known is termed as
   (a) Normal solution (b) Concentrate solution
   (c) Standard solution (d) Solvent
2. Solution which contains one gram eq. wt. of substance dissolved in one lit, of solution is known as
   (a) Molar solution (b) Normal solution
   (c) Molar solution (d) Standard solution
3. The gram equivalent weight of $Na_2 CO_3$ is
   (a) 40 (b) 53
   (c) 106 (d) 50
4. The gram equivalent weight of $H_2 SO_4$ is
   (a) 98 (b) 36.5
   (c) 49 (d) 63
5. One angstrom is equal to
   (a) 10^{-8} m (b) 10^{-9} m
   (c) 10^{-7} m (d) 10^{-10} m
6. One gram equivalent NaOH is equal to
   (a) 1000 mg NaOH (b) 40g NaOH
   (c) 4 g NaOH (d) 10000 mg NaOh
7. One milli equivalent NaOH is equal to
   (a) 40 mg NaOH (b) 40 g NaOH
   (c) 1000 mg NaOH (d) 10000 mg NaOH
8. Sodium chloride is a salt of
   (a) Strong acid – weak base (b) Weak acid – strong base
   (c) Strong acid – strong base (d) Weak acid – weak base
9. Basic it of $H_3 PO_4$ is
   (a) 1 (b) 2
   (c) 3 (d) 4

10. Acidity of Ca $(OH)_2$ is
(a) 1 (b) 2
(c) 3 (d) 4

11. Basicity of oxalic acid [H_2 C_2 O_4. $2H_2O$] is
(a) 1 (b) 2
(c) 2 (d) 3

12. Parts per million is equal to
(a) g/1 (b) mg/1
(c) g/kg (d) mg/ml

13. Oxidation reaction involves
(a) Loss of electrons (b) Gain of electrons
(c) Sharing of electrons (d) None of these

14. The example of oxidizing agent is
(a) NaC1 (b) $KMnO_4$
(c) $Ca(OH)_2$ (d) NaOH

15. The example of self indicator is
(a) Phenolphthalein (b) Methyl orange
(c) Methyl red (d) $KMnO_4$

16. The gram equivalent weight of $KMnO_4$ is
(a) 158 (b) 31.6
(c) 63.2 (d) 94.8

17. The glass electrode is used in
(a) pH meter (b) E.C. Meter
(c) Colorimeter (d) Spectrometer

18. Filter is used as dispersing device in
(a) Spectrometer (b) Colorimeter
(c) pH meter (d) E.C. Meter

19. Hemoglobin contains
(a) Nickel (b) Cobalt
(c) Magnesium (d) Iron

20. Fehling's B solution contains salt known as
(a) Raswlf salt (b) Benedict salt
(c) Rochelle salt (d) Rock salt

21. Vitamin C is also known as
(a) Acetic acid (b) Formic acid
(c) Ascorbic acid (d) Aspartic acid

22. Fehling's A solution contains
    (a) $FeSO_4$. $5H_2O$ (b) $MgSO_4$. $3H_2O$
    (c) $CuSO_4$. $5H_2O$ (d) $Zn5O_4$. $7H_2O$
23. Which vitamin contains metal ion?
    (a) Vitamin A (b) Vitamin C
    (c) Vitamin B_{12} (d) Vitamin B_1
24. Vitamin A deficiency causes
    (a) Scurvy (b) Beriberi
    (c) Night blindness (d) Dizziness
25. Sugar presents milk
    (a) Fructose (b) Galactose
    (c) Maltose (d) Lactose
26. The weight of a half mole of water is –
    (a) 9.0 gram (b) 1.0 gram
    (c) 0.5 gram (d) 18.0 gram
27. $_{17}Cl^{35}$ and $_{17}Cl^{37}$
    (a) isotopes (b) isobars
    (c) Isotones (d) isomer
28. An alpha particle consists of
    (a) Two neutrons (b) One neutrons
    (c) Two protons (d) Helium atom
29. Natural radioactivity was discovered by
    (a) Rutherford (b) Henri Becquerel
    (c) Mendeleeff's (d) Madame Curie
30. Le-chatelier's principle is apply only
    (a) System in equilibrium (b) System not in equilibrium
    (c) Heterrogenous reaction (d) Homogenous reaction
31. These element are kept in water
    (a) Sodium (b) potassium
    (c) Clorine (d) Nitrogen
32. Grouping of elements in periodic table is given by
    (a) Rutherford (b) Henri Becquerel
    (c) Mendeleeff's (d) Madame Curie
33. In the periodic table zero group contains
    (a) Transitionals elements (b) Alkaline earth
    (c) Rare earths (d) Inert elements

34. A solution containing 98 g of H_2SO_4 per litre will be
(a) Normal (b) Molar
(c) Centi normal (d) Hecta normal

35. Purity % of HCl
(a) 36 (b) 98
(c) 70 (d) None of these

36. Purity% of HNO_3
(a) 36 (b) 98
(c) 70 (d) None of these

37. Purity% of H_2SO_4
(a) 36 (b) 98
(c) 70 (d) None of these

38. Calculate the amount of chemical in 500 ml of $N/10$ NaCl
(a) 2.92 g (b) 1.82 g
(c) 20.12 g (d) 50 g

39. Calculate the amount of chemical in 500 ml of $N/10$ $MgCO_3$
(a) 2.92 g (b) 1.82 g
(c) 2.1 g (d) 50 g

40. Calculate the amount of chemical in 2 litre of 0.25 N KCl
(a) 2.92 g (b) 1.82 g
(c) 20.12 g (d) 37.25 g

41. Calculate the amount of chemical in 500 ml of 2% Nacl
(a) 10 g (b) 1.82 g
(c) 20.12 g (d) 50 g

42. 4% NaOH equal to .... Normal
(a) 10 N (b) 20 N
(c) 1 N (d) None of these

43. 20% $CaCl_2$ equal to .... Normal
(a) 10 N (b) 3.42 N
(c) 1 N (d) 2.72 N

44. A homogenous mixture of two or more substance is termed as
(a) Compound (b) Solution
(c) Mixture (d) All of these

45. The number of equivalent weights of a substance dissolved in 1 litre of a solution determines the.......
(a) Normality (b) Formality
(c) Molarity (d) Molality

46. The number of moles of a substance per litre of solution is called
    (a) Normality (b) Formality
    (c) Molarity (d) Molality
47. The number of moles per kilogram of water is called
    (a) Normality (b) Formality
    (c) Molarity (d) Molality
48. The number of moles of a substance per lkilogram of solution is called
    (a) Normality (b) Formality
    (c) Molarity (d) Molality

ANSWERS

1(c) 2(b) 3(b) 4(c) 5(d) 6(b) 7(a) 8(c) 9(c) 10(b) 11(b) 12(b) 13(a) 14(b) 15(d) 16(b) 17(a) 18(b) 19(d) 20(c) 21(c) 22(c) 23(c) 24(c) 25(d) 26(a) 27(a) 28(d) 29(b) 30(a) 31(c) 32(c) 33(d) 34(b) 35(a) 36(c) 37(b) 38(a) 39(c) 40(d) 41(a) 42(c) 43(d) 44(b) 45(a) 46(c) 47(d) 48(b)

CHAPTER - 2

Soil Physics

1. Father of Soil physics
   (a) Hillel (b) Richards
   (c) Dokuchaiev (d) Thomas Way
2. Theory of bonding of clay-clay particles given by
   (a) Thomas Way (b) Richards
   (c) E.J.Russel (d) Liebig
3. The book 'Fundamental of soil physics' was written by
   (a) Hillel (b) Richards
   (c) Dokuchaiev (d) Thomas Way
4. Major organic acid produced during decomposition of organic matter is
   (a) Polysaccharides (b) Humic acid
   (c) Fulvic acid (d) None of these
5. Naming of soil structure these following sequences is followed
   (a) Grade, class, type (b) Class, type, grade
   (c) Type, class, grade (d) Grade, type, class
6. Prismlike structure commonly found in
   (a) Sodic Soil (b) Humid soil
   (c) Saline soil (d) Arid and semi arid regions
7. The permeability classification of soil was given by
   (a) O Neal (b) Schofield
   (c) Atterberg (d) Chepil and Woodruff
8. 1 joule =
   (a) 10^5 ergs (b) 10^6 ergs
   (c) 10^7 ergs (d) 10^8 ergs
9. What is the unit of oxygen diffusion rate?
   (a) $g/cm^2/min$ (b) $min/cm^2/g$
   (c) cm/g/min (d) g/cm/min
10. The best agricultural texture is
    (a) Loam (b) Sand
    (c) Silt (d) Clay

11. The water retained by air dried soils is considered as
    (a) Gravitational (b) Hygroscopic
    (c) Capillary (d) Free
12. Natural soil aggregates are known as
    (a) Peds (b) Clods
    (c) Floccules (d) None of these
13. Soil pH is a measure of
    (a) Active acidity (b) Reserve acidity
    (c) Exchange acidity (d) None of these
14. Infiltration rate is relatively higher in
    (a) Sandy soil (b) Clay loam soil
    (c) Silty soil (d) Clay soil
15. Widely accepted fixed value of particle density is
    (a) 1.5 g/cc (b) 2.65 g/cc
    (c) 2.29 g/cc (d) 1.65 g/cc
16. The range of usefulness of tensiometer is between
    (a) 10-15 bar (b) 1-10 bar
    (c) 0.0-0.8 bar (d) -15 bar
17. Maximum density of water is at
    (a) 4°C (b) -4°C
    (c) 0°C (d) 10°C
18. The specific gravity of water
    (a) 1.5 Mgm^{-1} (b) 1.0 Mgm^{1}
    (c) 5.1 Mgm^{-1} (d) 0.1 Mgm^{-1}
19. The USDA sets the lower limit of soil to be what depth?
    (a) 3 feet (b) 2 meters
    (c) 5 feet (c) 1 km
20. Which term does not refer to a soil separate?
    (a) Sand (b) Loam
    (c) Silt (d) Clay
21. A soil with 35% clay and 35% sand would fit into which texture class?
    (a) Sandy (b) Loamy sand
    (c) Silty loam (d) Clay loam
22. Which textural class occupies the largest region on the textural triangle?
    (a) Loam (b) Silt loam
    (c) Sandy loam (d) Clay

23. Flat rock fragments of medium size are called
    (a) Cobbles (b) Flagstones
    (c) Gravel (d) Prisms
24. The first structure type to develop in a soil is usually:
    (a) Prismatic (b) Blocky
    (c) Platy (d) Rocky
25. Which element contributes to the deterioration of soil structure?
    (a) Calcium (b) Iron
    (c) Oxygen (d) Sodium
26. Which soil material would have the lowest bulk density?
    (a) Fragipan (b) Sandy loam
    (c) Silt loam (d) Peat
27. What is the approximate density of water?
    (a) 1000 mg/m^3 (b) 1 mg/m^3
    (c) 2.65 mg/m^3 (d) 3.14 mg/rn^3
28. Whether a soil is crumbly, firm, or rigid when wet is described by which term?
    (a) Thixotropy (b) Plasticity
    (c) Resistance to rupture (d) Stickiness
29. Compared with the atmosphere, soil air contains a lower concentration of which gas?
    (a) Oxygen (b) Nitrogen
    (c) Carbon dioxide (d) Water vapor
30. In a reduced soil when Eh values and oxygen concentrations are declining, which chemical becomes more abundant?
    (a) CO_2 (b) Fe^{2+}
    (c) MnO_2 (d) NO_{3-}
31. The value designation of a color indicates:
    (a) The amount of reflected light
    (b) The dominant spectral color
    (c) The purity of the color
    (d) The wavelength of light
32. The Earth receives most of its energy from the Sun in the form of:
    (a) Latent heat (b) Albedo
    (e) Long wave radiation (d) Short wave radiation
33. Which material will normally support weight best for engineering purposes such as building foundations?
    (a) Sand (b) Silt
    (c) Clay (d) Organic matter

34. The optimal water content for soil compaction is determined by which test?
    (a) Shrinkage test (b) Proctor test
    (c) Plasticity index (d) Liquid limit
35. The attraction between water and soil surfaces is described by which component of water potential?
    (a) Matric (b) Gravitational
    (c) Pressure (d) Osmotic
36. The effects of vertical position on the ability of water to do work is described by which component of water potential?
    (a) Matric (b) Gravitational
    (c) Pressure (d) Osmotic
37. The attraction between water and solid substances is called:
    (a) Adhesion (b) Cohesion
    (c) Friction (d) Saturation
38. If bulk density equals 1.5 mg/m^3, how will a soil's volumetric water content compare to its mass water content?
    (a) Bulk density is irrelevant to water content
    (b) Mass water content and volumetric water content will be equal
    (c) Mass water content will be greater than volumetric water content
    (d) Volumetric water content will be 1.5 times greater than mass water content
39. In unsaturated flow water moves:
    (a) From higher elevation to lower elevation
    (b) From higher potential to lower potential
    (c) From near a solid surface to further away from the surface
    (d) From clay to sand
40. Which of the water potential values below indicates water that is held most tightly soil?
    (a) -6000 kPa (b) -15000 kPa
    (c) -3 MPa (d) -33 kPa
41. Soil having which texture would normally have the smallest available water capacity?
    (a) Clay (b) Sand
    (c) Silt (d) Loam
42. Soil having which texture would normally have the greatest water content at any given water potential?
    (a) Sandy
    (b) Clay
    (c) Loamy
    (d) They would all have the same water content at a given water potential

43. Water movement into soil is controlled by:
(a) Soil texture (b) Soil structure
(c) Amount of water in the soil (d) All the above
44. Which material would normally have the greatest hydraulic conductivity?
(a) Gravel (b) Sand
(c) Loam (d) Clay
45. Which increasing evapo-transpiration ?
(a) Increasing wind (b) Increasing relative humidity
(c) Decreasing temperatures (d) Decreasing soil wetness
46. Follow is the practice of conserving water by:
(a) Mulching the soil (b) Fall plowing
(c) Fall irrigating (d) Leaving land unplanted
47. How dose deforestation affect the recycling of water on the land?
(a) After deforestation more water evaporates from the land land
(b) After deforestation more rain fall on the land
(c) After deforestation more water runs off the land
(d) Deforestation does not affect water cycling
48. How dose soil organic matters affect soil water content at field capacity?
(a) Increasing organic matter increases the water content
(b) Increasing organic matter decreases the water content
(c) Increasing organic matter increases deep percolation
(d) Organic matter has no influence on water content
49. A single clay particle might correctly be called a:
(a) Crystal (b) Colloid
(c) Micelle (d) All the above
50. The word clay refers to:
(a) A soil separate (b) A soil textural class
(c) A type of mineral (d) All the above
51. Why are clays less susceptible to erosion than silts and fine sands?
(a) Clays are smaller (b) Clays are better aggregated
(c) Clays are dryer (d) None of the above
52. Why are coarse sands less susceptible to erosion than silts and fine sands?
(a) Coarse sands are heavier
(b) Coarse sands are better aggregated
(c) Coarse sands are dryer
(d) None of the above

53. Which of the following factors related to the USLE are not manageable or changeable by the farmer?
    (a) C (b) R
    (c) LS (d) P
54. Why are cover crops rarely used in semiarid regions?
    (a) They do not control erosion (b) They deplete soil moisture
    (c) They do not grow very well (d) They violate local laws
55. Where does one find topographic deserts?
    (a) In the warm tropics
    (b) In the polar regions
    (c) On the west side of mountain ranges
    (d) On the east side of mountain ranges
56. Which factor in the wind erosion equation could a land manager readily control or alter?
    (a) I factor (b) C factor
    (c) V factor (d) None of the above
57. Which of the following statements is true regarding windbreaks?
    (a) They shelter natural predators (b) They produce fuel
    (c) They provide wildlife habitat (d) All the above
58. Successful irrigation depends on adequate:
    (a) Drainage (b) Salinity
    (c) Turbidity (d) Sodicity
59. Which factor is not a concern for irrigation water quality?
    (a) SAR (b) Salinity
    (c) Water hardness (d) Bicarbonates
60. Which substance below is not generally regarded as phytotoxic (toxic to plants) when present in irrigation water?
    (a) Sulfate (b) Bicarbonate
    (c) Chloride (d) Boron
61. The upper quarter of a plants rooting depth normally contains approximately what percentage of the plants roots ?
    (a) 25 (b) 10
    (c) 80 (d) 40
62. Which practice would allow more efficient use of water for irrigation?
    (a) Quit irrigating poorly responsive locations
    (b) Use drip or trickle systems
    (c) Replace open canals with pipelines
    (d) All the above

63. Why can an infrared thermometer be used to
    (a) One should always irrigate on hot days
    (b) When sprinkler water you need more of it
    (c) When crops are water stressed they get warmer
    (d) None of the above
64. Which of the following is not a problem associated specifically with furrow irrigation?
    (a) Run-of loss (b) Excessive evaporation
    (c) Furrow erosion (d) Deep percolation
65. Which type of sprinkler is especially well suited for sewage effluent because it dose not easily plug?
    (a) Large sprinkler guns (b) Center pivots
    (c) LEPA systems (d) Lateral-move lines
66. Which of the following poses the greatest challenge for drip irrigation?
    (a) The cost of water (b) Salinity in water
    (c) Plugging of emitters (d) The cost of labor
67. Which is not a problem specifically associated with irrigation on clay soils?
    (a) Excessive deep percolation (b) Poor aeration when wet
    (c) Slow infiltration (d) Difficult field operations
68. The new term micro irrigation refers to which method?
    (a) Small sprinklers (b) Small furrows
    (c) Greenhouse irrigation (d) Drip irrigation
69. The weight of produce grown per volume of water used is a measure of:
    (a) Leaching (b) Water potential
    (c) Water use efficiency (d) None of the above
70. A wind uprooting a tree growing on a shallow, wet soil is an example of the failure of the soil to provide sufficient to the tree's roots.
    (a) Physical support (b) Temperature moderation
    (c) Nutrient elements (d) Protection from toxins
71. Which type of irrigation system usually achieves the greatest "field water efficiency?
    (a) Level basin irrigation
    (b) Furrow irrigation
    (c) Center pivot automated sprinkler irrigation
    (d) Micro or drip irrigation

72. According to International Classification of soil particle, the size of silt particle should be
    (a) 0.02-0.002 mm (b) 0.001-0.0002 mm
    (c) 0.2-0.002 mm (d) Less than 0.0002 min
73. According to U.S.D.A soil classification the size of sand particle is
    (a) 0.001-0.0002 (b) 0.02-0002 mm
    (c) 0.02-2 mm (d) Less than 0.002 mm
74. According to U.S.D.A soil classification the size of clay particle should be
    (a) 0.02-0002 mm (b) 0.2-2 mm
    (c) Less than 0.002 mm (d) None of the above
75. Distinguished set of operation of soil and water conservation project is/are
    (a) Planning and executing measure to check erosion, improved land productivity and reclaim waste land
    (b) The mapping of land for classification according to its capability
    (c) Both of the above
    (d) None of the above
76. Black and dark coloured soils absorb heat from sun light than light
    (a) More (b) Less
    (c) Negligible (d) Very high
77. Which of the following in not a kind of soil structure'
    (a) Compact (b) Columner
    (c) Granular (d) None of these
78. Which of the following soil texture is lighter than others
    (a) Sandy loam (b) Clay loam
    (c) Silty clay loam (d) Loamy sand
79. Which of the following soil texture is heavier than others
    (a) Loamy sand (b) Loam
    (c) Silt clay loam (d) Silty loam
80. The amount of work done by the water during its movement from initial point to reference point is known as
    (a) Solute water potential (b) Matric potential
    (c) Soil water potential (d) Pressure potential
81. The percentage of soil water held with water potential-15 bars is called as
    (a) Field capacity (b) Hygroscopic coefficient
    (c) Wilting point (d) None of the above

82. V=2rg (PP-Pm) /gn is
(a) Darcy's law (b) stock's law
(c) Beer's law (d) None of these
83. DQ = DA (Dc/dx) dt is the
(a) Fick's law of diffusion (b) Stock's law
(c) Darcy's law (d) None of the above
84. Q=Ki is the ... equation
(a) Stock's law (b) Darcy's equation
(c) Fick's law (d) None of the above
85. Q = KA(P-P_1)/ni Denotes the -
(a) Stock's law of velocity of falling
(b) Fick's law of diffusion
(c) Darcy's equation of gas flow
(d) None of the above
86. The ratio of thermal conductivity and heat capacity is known as
(a) Thermal diffusivity (b) Heat capacity
(c) Thermal capacity (d) None of the above
87. A soil absorbs about of incoming solar radiation
(a) 5% (b) 10%
(c) 15% (d) 20%
88. The global average of solar radiation reaching the earth is
(a) 20% (b) 30%
(c) 40% (d) 50%
89. The prime objective of conservation tillage is
(a) Partial retention of plant residues
(b) Complete retention of plant residues
(c) Removal of plant residues
(d) None of these
90. In no tillage systems, the surface soil layers have
(a) Higher total pore space (b) Lower bulk density ?
(c) Higher bulk density (d) Lower water infiltration
91. Conservation tillage tends to encourage
(a) Reduced soil fauna (b) Lower number of earthworms
(c) High microbial population (d) None of these
92. Wind laden with soil particles embodies the abrasive action which is
(a) Greatly increased (b) Greatly decreased
(c) Absolutely unaffected (d) None of these

93. The diameter of most erodible soil particles is
    (a) 0.2 mm (b) 0.3 mm
    (c) 0.4 (d) 0.1 mm
94. Cost-sharing assistance for soil conservation had been in practice for years in
    (a) England (b) India
    (c) U.S.A. (d) China
95. Before transplanting of paddy, puddling is done
    (a) To increase the percolation of water in soil
    (b) To reduce the percolation of water in soil
    (c) To increase the availability of nutrients
    (d) To increase the activity of micro-organisms
96. The movement of nutrients or ions by mass flow is reduced at low temperature
    (a) Low respiration (b) Low transpiration
    (c) Low photosynthesis (d) None of these
97. Hydraulic conductivity is increased with
    (a) Increase in pore size (b) Decrease in pore size
    (c) a and b both (d) None of the above
98. Work is a
    (a) Force × distance (b) Distance/sec
    (c) Force/unit (d) None of these
99. pF is unit of
    (a) Force (b) Distance
    (c) Velocity (d) Weight
100. Specific heat of soil water
    (a) 1.0 calories/g (b) 0.40 calories/g
    (c) 0.5 calories/g (d) 0.22 calories/g
101. Specific heat of humus
    (a) 1.0 calories/g (b) 0.40 calories/g
    (c) 0.5 calories/g (d) 0.22 calories/g
102. Specific heat of ice
    (a) 1.0 calories/g (b) 0.40 calories/g
    (c) 0.5 calories/g (d) 0.22 calories/g
103. Specific heat of clay soil
    (a) 1.0 calories/g (b) 0.40 calories/g
    (c) 0.5 calories/g (d) 0.22 calories/g

104. Specific heat of dry mineral soil
(a) 1.0 calories/g (b) 0.40 calories/g
(c) 0.5 calories/g (d) 0.22 calories/g

105. How much heat is required for vaporization of 1 gm water at 20° C
(a) 500 calories (b) 540 calories
(c) 550 calories (d) 450 calories

106. Which of the following gas is the highest concentration in soil
(a) CO_2 (b) N_2
(c) O_2 (d) SO_2

107. Gypsum blocks can measure the soil water potential up to
(a) 1-15 bar (b) 15-31 bar
(c) 31-1000 bar (d) less than 1 bar

108. Which of the following is not used for measuring soil water
(a) Tensiometer (b) Zypsum block
(c) Pressure bomb (d) Neutron meter

109. Which of the following is the source of neutrons in neutron moisture meter
(a) Radium (b) Thorium
(c) P^{32} (d) Iodine

110. Which of the following cannot prevent the soil water loss
(a) Mulch (b) Hexadecanol
(c) Wind breakers (d) Deforestation

111. Saturated flow can be expressed by following law
(a) Darcy's law (b) Newton's law
(c) Law of mass action (d) None of these

112. Pascal is a unit of
(a) Water potential (b) Velocity
(c) Work (d) Distance

113. Munshel soil colour chart is used for measuring the
(a) Light colour (b) Water potential
(c) Sewage colour (d) Soil colour

114. The root growth of crops stops completely at bulk density of soil
(a) 1.2-1.6 g/cc (b) 1.4-1.5 g/cc
(c) 1.7-1.9 g/cc (d) None of these

115. Climate was first classified
(a) De Candole (b) Marbut
(c) Coffey (d) Mitscherlich

116. International Institute of Tropical Agriculture is situated in
    (a) India (b) Nigeria
    (c) Australia (d) South africa
117. Climate classification based on weather elements was made by
    (a) Coffey (b) N.V.Kantikar
    (c) Koppen (d) Leather
118. Broad bed and furrow system is followed in
    (a) Black soil (b) Peat soil
    (c) Waterlogged soil (d) Red soil
119. Which type of plants is more drought tolerant
    (a) C4 (b) C3
    (c) Both a and b (d) CAM
120. World water day is celebrated on
    (a) January 22 (b) October 16
    (c) March 22 (d) December 1
121. Percentage of water used for metabolic process of crop is
    (a) Less than 1 (b) 10%
    (c) 20% (d) 40%
122. Father of Tillage
    (a) Liebig (b) Marbut
    (c) Koppen (d) Jethrotull
123. What is the oxygen diffusion rate (ODR) for most crops
    (a) 20×10^{-8} gm/cm^2/min (b) 18×10^{-8} gm/cm^2/min
    (c) 22×10^{-8} gm/cm^2/min (d) 20×10^{-6} gm/cm^2/min
124. Wheat grows best at
    (a) 35° C (b) 15° C
    (c) 40° C (d) 24° C
125. The presence of water films between particles improve thermal contact and increase
    (a) Thermal conductivity (b) Specific heat
    (c) Heat of vaporization (d) All of these
126. Capillary rise of water is measured by the formula h=
    (a) 0.15/r (b) 0.35/r
    (c) 0.25/r (d) 0.10/r
127. Unit of surface tension
    (a) Poise (b) dynes/cm
    (c) g/cc (d) cm/s

128. In the field hydraulic conductivity is measured by
   (a) Mechanical analysis (b) Piezometer
   (c) Constant head permeameter (d) Auger hole method
129. In the field hydraulic conductivity is measured by
   (a) Mechanical analysis (b) Piezometer
   (c) Constant head permeameter (d) Auger hole method
130. Unit of hydraulic conductivity
   (a) cm/sec^2 (b) cm/sec
   (c) kg/ha (d) Poise
131. Permeability classification is given by
   (a) Sorenson (b) Marbut
   (c) Hillel (d) O Neal
132. In Munsell soil colour chart Hue denotes
   (a) Wavelength of light (b) Reflection of light
   (c) Purity of colour (d) All of these
133. In Munsell soil colour chart Chroma denotes
   (a) Wavelength of light (b) Reflection of light
   (c) Purity of colour (d) All of these
134. In Munsell soil colour chart Hue number zero indicate
   (a) White (b) Black
   (c) Red (d) Yellow
135. In Munsell soil colour chart Hue number 10 indicate
   (a) White (b) Black
   (c) Red (d) Yellow
136. In Munsell soil colour chart Value number zero indicate
   (a) White (b) Black
   (c) Red (d) Yellow
137. In Munsell soil colour chart Value number 10 indicate
   (a) White (b) Black
   (c) Red (d) Yellow
138. In Munsell soil colour chart Range of Hue
   (a) 0-10 (b) 1-10
   (c) 1-9 (d) 0-9
139. In Munsell soil colour chart Range of Value
   (a) 0-10 (b) 1-10
   (c) 1-9 (d) 0-9

140. In Munsell soil colour chart Range of Chroma
    (a) 0-10 (b) 1-10
    (c) 1-9 (d) 0-8
141. The value of diffusion coefficient
    (a) 0.0-2.0 (b) 0.5-0.9
    (c) 0.6-0.8 (d) 1.0-1.5
142. One cusec is equal to
    (a) 28.32 litre (b) 29.32 litre
    (c) 30.32 litre (d) 27.32 litre
143. The value of pF at wilting point
    (a) 4.50 (b) 4.28
    (c) 4.18 (d) 2.53
144. The value of pF at hygroscopic point
    (a) 4.50 (b) 4.28
    (c) 4.18 (d) 2.53
145. The value of pF at oven dry condition
    (a) 4.50 (b) 7.00
    (c) 4.18 (d) 2.53
146. The value of pF at field capacity
    (a) 4.50 (b) 4.28
    (c) 4.18 (d) 2.53
147. The value of pF at saturated condition
    (a) 4.50 (b) 4.28
    (c) Zero (d) 2.53
148. Ratio of volume of air and solids of soil is known as
    (a) Void ratio (b) Porosity
    (c) Particle density (d) Bulk density
149. Sodium (Na) is utilized essentially by the ... crop
    (a) Okra (b) Cabbage
    (c) Cauliflower (d) Knol-khol
150. Canopy temperature is measured by
    (a) Infra red thermometer (b) Irrometer
    (c) Hygrometer (d) Tensionmeter
151. Hydraulic conductivity of soils varies directly with
    (a) Total porosity (b) Water holding capacity
    (c) Capillary porosity (d) Non-capillary porosity

152. Amount of heat required to raise temperature of 1 gm soil from 14 to 15° C is known
(a) Thermal conductivity (b) Head capacity
(c) Specific heat (d) None of the above

153. Soil structural units having horizontal axis much longer than vertical axis. Such type of soil structure is known as
(a) Platy (b) Blocky
(c) Prismatic (d) Columnar

154. The arrangement of the different soil aggregates
(a) Soil structure (b) Soil texture
(c) Soil consistence (d) Soil dispersion

155 At field capacity moisture is held at
(a) 31 atm (b) 1 atm
(c) 1/3 atm (d) None known

156. Gravitational potential in soil water is potential created due to
(a) Mass of the soil solids (b) Presence of organic matter in soil
(c) Soil solution (d) Gravity

157. If the particle size is 2 mm to 7.5 cm than it is known as:
(a) Silt (b) Stones
(c) Gravels (d) Sand

158. Which of the following primary minerals has no good and nutrient holding capacity:
(a) Feldspar (b) Mica
(c) Quartz (d) All of these

159. Lithosphere has about igneous rocks
(a) 75% (b) 95%
(c) 80% (d) 72%

160. Which one of the following sets of soil conditions is more suitable for plant growth?
(a) Sandy soils with high aeration and low water holding capacity
(b) Clay soils with high water holding capacity and low aeration
(c) Organic soils with high water holding capacity and low
(d) Loamy soils with medium aeration aeration and medium water holding capacity

161. Soils containing high proportion of organic matter have the following colour
(a) Dark colour (b) Red colour
(c) Yellow colour (d) Light colour

162. Relative proportion of soil separates in sand, silt and clay is termed as
    (a) Soil texture (b) Soil structure
    (c) Soil porosity (d) None of these
163. The arrangement of individual soil particles in a specific pattern is called
    (a) Soil texture (b) Soil structure
    (c) Soil separates (d) None of these
164. The pore space in a soil is usually partly filled with
    (a) Humus (b) Clay
    (c) Water (d) Silt
165. The amount of hydrogen ions (H) in the soil solution is indicated by the
    (a) Eh (b) Texture
    (c) H-index (d) pH
166. The mineral portion of a soil is comprised (by weight) of 23% clay and 55% sand. What is the percentage that consists of silt?
    (a) 78% (b) 32%
    (c) 22% (d) 39%
167. Which type of soil structure features mainly horizontal interped cracks (planar pores) that tend to inhibit downward root growth ?
    (a) Angular block (b) Columnar
    (c) Granular (d) Platy
168. Water flow by capillary movement toward a plant root is an example of
    (a) Saturated flow (b) Unsaturated flow
    (c) Vapor movement (d) Osmotic potential
169. Soil is said to be at "field capacity" when
    (a) The total soil water potential =0
    (b) The total soil water potential is 33.0 kPa
    (c) The volume water content is 25%
    (d) Gravitational drainage has nearly ceased
170. Preferential or bypass water flow usually occurs
    (a) In earthworm channels, cracks, or other macropores
    (b) In confined aquifers
    (c) In the micropores of fine textured soils
    (d) During light rainfall that continues for several hours
171. Approximate distance of the ozone layer is
    (a) 100-120 km (b) 60-80 km
    (c) 120-140 km (d) 80-100 km

172. A hardpan forming at or just below the normal depth of tillage is called
(a) Plow pan (b) Bottom pan
(c) Clay pan (d) Fragipan
173. Which of the following tools consists of several sweeps pulled crop rows to cut and kill weeds
(a) Moldboard (b) Chisel
(c) Cultivator (d) Rotary plow
174. The most strong and heavy planters are needed for which type of farming?
(a) Conventional (b) No-till
(c) Reduced tillage (d) Conservation
175. Which soils, especially in cold climates, are least adaptable to reduce tillage?
(a) Loamy (b) Silty
(c) Clayey (d) Sandy
176. In much of the world farming techniques have not changed in centuries because of
(a) Cultural contraints (b) Financial contraints
(c) Technological constraints (d) All the above
177. Which of the following is a benefit of reduced tilage ?
(a) Decreased compaction (b) Decreased erosion
(c) Decreased fuel use (d) All the above
178. Compared with conventional tillage fields at the time of planting, reduced tillage tend do be:
(a) Warmer (b) Cooler
(c) Drier (d) Cleaner
179. Which crop produces nonagile residues?
(a) Cotton (b) Peanuts
(c) Wheat (d) Soybeans
180. Which is not considered one of the four main tools (or practices) for soil conservation?
(a) Conservation tillages (b) Pesticides
(c) Vegetative (d) Genetic engineering
181. Among the following types of soil water which one is the most useful for the plants
(a) Capillary water (b) Gravitational water
(c) Combined water (d) Hygroscopic water

182. At what level of atmospheric pressure free flowing of water is available
   (a) <1/3 atmosphere pressure (b) <2/3 atmosphere pressure
   (c) >1/3 atmosphere pressure (d) None of the above
183. The concentration of carbon dioxide found is the soil is
   (a) 0.90% (b) 0.25%
   (c) 0.75% (d) 0.95%
184. Amount of water in 1 cubic meter means
   (a) 10 litres (b) 1000 litres
   (c) 10,000 (d) 100 litres
185. Water use efficiency is defined as
   (a) Economic yield per unit of irrigation water applied
   (b) Ratio of water used by the crop to the irrigation water applied
   (c) Ratio of net irrigation to gross irrigation including other losses
   (d) Dry matter produced per unit of water used by the crop
186. Gross water requirement of a crop is the
   (a) Total available water, which is present in the soil profile during the crop period
   (b) Same as total rainfall in the crop period under heavy rainfall areas
   (c) Evaporation and water used by crop for its metabolic activities
   (d) Sum of net irrigation requirement effective rainfall and other unavoidable during irrigation
187. Tillage of the soil rate of disappearance of organic matter
   (a) Increases (b) Maintains
   (c) Reduces (d) Has no effect
188. Which of the following are metamorphic rocks
   (a) Schist (b) Slate
   (c) Dolomite (d) Shales
189. Per cent pore space can not be calculated correctly by
   (a) $\%\text{ pore space} = \frac{\text{Bulk density}}{\text{Particle density}} \times 100$
   (b) % pore space = 100% solid
   (c) $\%\text{ pore space} = \frac{\text{Bulk density}}{\text{Particle density}} \times 100$
   (d) $\%\text{ pore space} = \frac{\text{Bulk density}}{2.65\text{ g/cm}^3} \times 100$

190. The efficiency of field irrigation would be more in
(a) Sandy loam (b) Loam
(c) Clay loam (d) Heavy loam

191. Which one of the following occupies the highest volume percent in a fine sandy loam surface soil in good condition, for plant growth?
(a) Organic mailer
(b) Mineral mailer
(c) Pore space which includes air and/or water
(d) Others including macro nd micro flora and fauna

192. The diameter of very fine sand particles is
(a) Below 0.002 mm (b) 0.05 to 0.10 mm
(c) Below 0.02 mm (d) 0.01-0.05 mm

193. The mineral weathering and clay formation are rapid where the climate is
(a) Warm and moist (b) Warm and dry
(c) Cold and dry (d) Cold and moist

194. Soil water content (%) at field capacity is maximum/highest with
(a) Loam (b) Silt loam
(c) Clayey soils (d) Clay loam

195. Which of the following soils has got the highest bulk density
(a) Clay Soil (b) Silty clay
(c) Loam (d) Sand soil

196. The diameter of the silt particles is
(a) 0.0005-0.0002 (b) 0.5 to 0.2 mm
(c) Less than 0.002 (d) 0.05-0.002

197. Different soil separate may be determined with the help of
(a) Yet's chart (b) Munsell chart
(c) International pipette method (d) None of the above

198. The arrangement of small medium and large soil particles in set patterns is known as
(a) Mean weight diameter (b) Particle density
(c) Soil texture (d) Soil structure

199. The natural soil aggregates are called as
(a) Soil separates (b) Mottling
(c) Peds (d) Concretion

200. The average soil bulk density of cultivated loamy soil is approximately
(a) 1.5-1.65 gm cm^{-3} (b) 1.1-1.4 gm cm^{-3}
(c) 1.5-1.0 cm cm^{-3} (d) None of the above

201. The mass per unit volume of the solid mass of the soil excluding pore space is known
(a) True density (b) Bulk density
(c) a and b both (d) None of these

202. Organic matter content of histosols' and hydromorphic soil is
(a) 30-40% (b) 2-18%
(c) 50-57% (d) 60-70%

203. The relative amounts of air and water in the pore spaces
(a) Half filled and half empty (b) Always remain constant
(c) Fluctuate continuously (d) All of the above

204. Moisture content from lower to upper plastic limit is known as
(a) Sticky point (b) Plastic number
(c) Field capacity (d) All the above

205. Soil colour determination is standardized and determined by the comparison of the soil colour to
(a) Tenslo meter (b) Munsell chart
(c) Gypsum block (d) None of these

206. 'Hue' is the term which is used for the determination of
(a) Dominant spectral or rainbow
(b) Relative thickness of whiteness
(c) Purity of the colour
(d) All of the above

207. The main source of heat energy for soil is
(a) Infrared radiation (b) Solar radiation
(c) Altra violet radiation (d) None of the above

208. Specific heat of the mineral matter is
(a) 1.0 cal gm^{-1} (b) 24.0 cal gm^{-1}
(c) 0.462 cal gm^{-1} (d) 0.187 Cal gm^{-1}

209. Temperature has not significant effects on
(a) Structure
(b) Weathering of rocks and minerals
(c) Biologicl activity
(d) .411 of the above

210. Decomposition of organic matter, cycling of nutrient mcluding addition of nitrogen, which are vitally important process in soil formation are made possible by present of
(a) Soil pH (b) Soil minerals
(c) Soil colloids (d) Soil microbes

211. Soil is biochemically withered part of
(a) Parent material (b) Organic matter
(c) Regolith (d) Bedrock
212. A mass of unconsolidated debris varying in composition from place to place and covering bedrock is defined as
(a) Soil horizon (b) Soil debris
(c) Regolith (d) Soil profile
213. Quartzite are metamorphic rocks derived from
(a) Slate (b) Granite
(c) Limestone (d) Qurtz
214. Alluvial soils in India are:
(a) Very rare (b) Most extensive soils
(c) Found desert (d) Lease fertile
215. There is a net increase m the mineralization of organic nitrogen in soil when:
(a) C:N ratio is below 20:1
(b) C:N ratio is above 30:1
(c) Nitrogen is taken up by the crops
(d) C:N ratio is 20 to 30.1
216. Hydraulic conductivity of soils varies directly with
(a) Total porosity (b) Water holding capacity
(c) Capillary porosity (d) Non-capillary porosity
217. Amount of heat required to raise temperature of 1 gm soil from 14 to 15° C is known as
(a) Thermal conductivity (b) Head capacity
(c) Specific heat (d) None of the above
218. Soil structural units having horizontal axis much longer than vertical axis. Such type of soil structure is known as
(a) Platy (b) Blocky
(c) Prismatic (d) None of the above
219. The arrangement of the different soil aggregates
(a) Soil structure (b) Soil texture
(c) Soil consistence (d) Soil dispersion
220. At field capacity moisture is held at
(a) 31 atm (b) 1 atm
(c) 1/3 atm (d) None known
221. Specific heat of the dry soil is equal to
(a) 0.2 al/gm (b) 1.0 al/gm
(c) 0.5 al/gm (d) None of these

222. Gravitational potential in soil water is potential
    (a) Mass of the soil solids (b) Presence of organic matter in soil
    (c) Soil solution (d) Gravity
223. Relative proportion of soil separates in sand, silt and clay is termed as
    (a) Soil texture (b) Soil structure
    (c) Soil porosity (d) None of these
224. The arrangement of individual soil particles in a specific pattern is called
    (a) Soil texture (b) Soil structure
    (c) Soil separates (d) None of these
225. The alkali soil have an excess of
    (a) Calcium (b) Sodium
    (c) Zinc (d) Potassium

ANSWERS

1(a) 2(c) 3(a) 4(b) 5(a) 6(d) 7(a) 8(c) 9(a) 10(a) 11(b) 12(a) 13(a) 14(a) 15(b) 16(c) 17(a) 18(b) 19(b) 20(b) 21(d) 22(d) 23(b) 24(a) 25(d) 26(d) 27(b) 28(c) 29(a) 30(b) 31(a) 32(d) 33(a) 34(b) 35(a) 36(b) 37(a) 38(d) 39(b) 40(a) 41(b) 42(b) 43(d) 44(a) 45(a) 46(a) 47(c) 48(a) 49(d) 50(d) 51(b) 52(a) 53(b) 54(b) 55(d) 56(d) 57(d) 58(a) 59(c) 60(a) 61(d) 62(d) 63(c) 64(b) 65(a) 66(c) 67(a) 68(d) 69(c) 70(a) 71(d) 72(a) 73(c) 74(c) 75(b) 76(a) 77(d) 78(d) 79(c) 80(c) 81(c) 82(a) 83(a) 84(b) 85(c) 86(a) 87(b) 88(d) 89(a) 90(c) 91(c) 92(a) 93(d) 94(c) 95(b) 96(b) 97(a) 98(a) 99(a) 100(a) 101(b) 102(c) 103(d) 104(d) 105(b) 106(b) 107(a) 108(c) 109(a) 110(d) 111(a) 112(a) 113(d) 114(c) 115(a) 116(b) 117(c) 118(d) 119(d) 120(c) 121(a) 122(d) 123(a) 124(d) 125(a) 126(a) 127(b) 128(b) 129(c) 130(b) 131(d) 132(a) 133(c) 134(c) 135(d) 136(b) 137(a) 138(a) 139(a) 140(d) 141(c) 142(a) 143(c) 144(a) 145(b) 146(d) 147(c) 148(a) 149(c) 150(a) 151(d) 152(c) 153(a) 154(a) 155(c) 156(d) 157(c) 158(c) 159(b) 160(d) 161(a) 162(a) 163(b) 164(c) 165(d) 166(c) 167(d) 168(b) 169(d) 170(a) 171(a) 172(a) 173(c) 174(b) 175(c) 176(d) 177(d) 178(b) 179(c) 180(d) 181(a) 182(a) 183(b) 184(b) 185(d) 186(d) 187(a) 188(b) 189(a) 190(c) 191(c) 192(d) 193(a) 194(d) 195(a) 196(d) 197(c) 198(d) 199(c) 200(b) 201(a) 202(b) 203(c) 204(b) 205(b) 206(a) 207(b) 208(d) 209(a) 210(d) 211(c) 212(c) 213(d) 214(b) 215(a) 216(d) 217(c) 218(a) 219(a) 220(c) 221(a) 222(d) 223(a) 224(b) 225(b)

CHAPTER - 3

Soil Pedology

1. The metamorphic rock formed due to action of high pressure is known as
   (a) Dynamo metamorphic (b) Thermo metamorphic
   (c) Hydro metamorphic (d) None of these
2. Horizon B_2 is also known as
   (a) Illuvial horizon (b) Eluvial horizon
   (c) Solum (d) Transition horizon
3. Hematite is converted to limonite by the process of
   (a) Hyadration (b) Hydrolysis
   (c) Oxidation (d) Carbonation
4. The order of desert soil is
   (a) Entisoils (b) Aridisols
   (c) Vertisols (d) Inceptisols
5. According to LCC, which class of land is suitable for wild life?
   (a) II (b) VI
   (c) IV (d) VIII
6. Which is a secondary mineral?
   (a) Mica (b) Hornblende
   (c) Feldspar (d) Silicate clay
7. Which soil forming factor becomes increasingly dominant over time because of its effects on other factors?
   (a) Climate (b) Parent material
   (c) Relief (d) Organisms
8. When a soil begins to undergo profile changes because of weathering and leaching the original materials in which these changes occur are:
   (a) Landforms (b) Sediments
   (c) Parent materials (d) Residual soils
9. Sediments deposited from flowing water are called:
   (a) Organic soil (b) Peat soil
   (c) Mineral soils (d) Alluvium

10. Older flood plains at higher levels than the river bottoms are called:
    (a) Deltas (b) River terraces
    (c) Bluffs (d) Plateaus
11. Sediments deposited in standing fresh water are called:
    (a) Marine deposits (b) Flood plains
    (c) Lacustrine deposits (d) Eolian deposits
12. The general name for glacial deposits is:
    (a) Glacial hills (b) Loess hills
    (c) Plains (d) Loam
13. Which is not considered a soil forming factor?
    (a) Topography (b) Time
    (c) Sedimentation (d) Climate
14. Which subsoil master horizon contains accumulations of small particles like clays and salts?
    (a) A (b) B
    (c) C (d) R
15. Which is the term used to designate an eluvial horizon?
    (a) A (b) B
    (c) C (d) E
16. Which subsoil horizon is a brittle hardpan?
    (a) Fragipan (b) Duripan
    (c) Petrocalcic (d) Kandic
17. A GIS might include which attribute?
    (a) Rainfall (b) Elevation
    (c) Soil type (d) All the above
18. Which professionals employ GPS in their work?
    (a) Soldiers (b) Fishermen
    (c) Soil scientists (d) All the above
19. A group of pedons linked together is called a:
    (a) Triplepedon (b) Multipedon
    (c) Polypedon (d) Taxopedon
20. Soils of which order always has a subsoil accumulation of clay i.e., argillic horizon?
    (a) Oxisols (b) Ultisols
    (c) Andisols (d) Gelisols
21. Which soil temperature regime describes soils with limited moisture, but with moisture present during the growing season?
    (a) Udic (b) Xeric
    (c) Ustic (d) Aridic

22. Which is the most common soil order in the world?
    (a) Entisols (b) Mollisols
    (c) Oxisols (d) Alfisols
23. Soils of the suborder Histels belong to which soil order?
    (a) Geisols (b) Histosols
    (c) Inceptisols (d) None of the above
24. Which would be most suitable for Histosols?
    (a) Urban development (b) Orchards
    (c) Onions (d) Corn
25. Certain formative elements describe conditions that would never apply to certain soil orders. With this in mind, which of the following suborders exists?
    (a) Cryox (b) Udids
    (c) Xererts (d) Torrods
26. Which is the warmest soil temperature regime?
    (a) Mesic (b) Thermic
    (c) Hyperthermic (d) Cryic
27. Which of the following is the most common use for Gelisols?
    (a) Root crops (b) Wildlife habitat
    (c) Urban development (d) Pineapple crops
28. An example of a soil constituent that is considered to be part of the biosphere is
    (a) Soil solution (b) Humus
    (c) Clay (d) Sand
29. An example if a soil constituent that is part of the lithosphere is
    (a) Soil solution (b) Humus
    (c) Clay (d) Carbon dioxide
30. In a soil that contains all of these horizons, which one would be on the top?
    (a) A horizon (b) B horizon
    (c) O horizon (d) E horizon
31. In a soil that contained all of these horizons, which would be on the bottom?
    (a) A (b) B
    (c) C (d) E
32. Pedologists study the entire soil profile, but on general they show less interest in the horizon than do edaphologists.
    (a) A (b) B
    (c) C (d) E

33. Which of the following horizons is usually considered to be subsoil?
    (a) A (b) B
    (c) C (d) E
34. Compared to the B horizon, the A horizon is likely to be higher in
    (a) Clay (b) Organic flatter
    (c) Unweathered rock (d) Carbonates
35. Letters such as Bt. Ck, Bs. Ap, and Eg designate
    (a) Pedons (b) Diagnostic horizons
    (c) Genetic horizons (d) Soil orders
36. Epi-aquic soil conditions may be caused by the presence of
    (a) A subsoil layer of sand and gravel
    (b) An impermeable clay layer
    (c) A fragipan layer
    (d) All of the above
37. A "soil association" is a group of about 3 to 10 different soils that......
    (a) Belong to the same soil Family
    (b) Belong to the same soil order
    (c) Have the same surface horizon texture
    (d) Regularly occur together in the landscape
38. A .... is a group of soils formed on the same parent material but differing in internal drainage class because of their slope position
    (a) Soil Family (b) Soil association
    (c) Soil union (d) Soil catena
39. Granite and basalt are:
    (a) Sedimentary (b) Igneous rock
    (c) Metamorphic (d) None of the above
40. Feldspar is a:
    (a) Primary mineral (b) Secondary mineral
    (c) Accessory mineral (d) Clay mineral
41. Basic colour of vertisols is due to presence of
    (a) Titanium (b) Selenium
    (c) Organic matter (d) Monimorillonite clay
42. The weathering causes
    (a) Disintegration and decomposition of rocks
    (b) Disintegration of rocks
    (c) Disintegration and decomposition
    (d) Both a and c of minerals

43. In chemical weathering the Composition of minerals –
    (a) Remain the same as in original rocks
    (b) Unaffected
    (c) Changed
    (d) None of the above
44. Weathered material transported by means of force of gravity the deposition is termed as
    (a) Cumulose (b) Aeolion
    (c) Alluvial (d) Colluvial
45. The weathered material transported by means of waters and deposited in river basins are termed as
    (a) Alluvial (b) Lacustrine
    (c) Marine (d) None of these
46. Soil survey's are mainly of different types
    (a) Three types (b) Four types
    (c) Two types (d) None of these
47. Green red and blue colour lands belong to classes, I, II and IV suitable for
    (a) Pasture
    (b) Cultivated crops
    (c) Forests and wild life food and cover
    (d) All of these
48. Water resources are utilized mainly for –
    (a) Irrigation (b) Domestic water supply
    (c) Industrial (d) All of the above
49. Green colour land, belongs class 1 is –
    (a) Nearly level, deep, well-drained, hold water well
    (b) Erosion hazard low
    (c) Both of the above
    (d) None of the above
50. Which one of the following sets of soil conditions is more suitable for plant growth
    (a) Organic soil with high water holding capacity with low aeration
    (b) Sandy soils with high aeration and low water holding capacity
    (c) Clay soils with higher water holding capacity with low aeration
    (d) Loamy soils with medium aeration and medium water holding capacity

51. Jhuming is a system of
    (a) Shifting cultivation of the steep deforested hilly slopes
    (b) Conserving soil and moisture
    (c) Wind erosion for destroying the valuable top soil in many areas
    (d) None of the above
52. The orders of laterite soil are
    (a) Ultisol (b) Alfisol
    (c) Oxisol (d) Both a and c
53. 'Detailed soil survey' the base maps used having scale
    (a) 1″: 1 mile (b) 1″: 8 mile
    (c) 1″: 16 mile (d) None of these
54. The new comprehensive soil classification is based on
    (a) Physical and chemical properties of soil
    (b) Genetic characters
    (c) a and b both
    (d) None of the above
55. B horizon of the soil is designated as
    (a) Illuviated horizon (b) Eluviated horizon
    (c) a and b both (d) None of the above
56. The rock which is formed by cooling and solidification of molten magma is
    (a) Sedimentary rock (b) Metamorphic rock
    (c) Igneous rock (d) None of the above
57. Granite is a............ rock
    (a) Sedimentary (b) Metamorphic
    (c) Igneous (d) None of these
58. The rock which is formed by sedimentation of primary rock, is called
    (a) Sedimentary rock (b) Igneous rock
    (c) Metamorphic rock (d) None of the above
59. Sand stone and lime stone are the example of... rock
    (a) Metamorphic (b) Sedimentary
    (c) Igneous (d) All of these
60. The rock which is formed under high temperature and pressure and by sudden geological tectonic movement, is called
    (a) Igneous rock (b) Metamorphic rock
    (c) Sedimentary rock (d) None of the above

61. Quartzite is an example of .... rock –
(a) Sedimentary (b) Igneous
(c) Metamorphic (d) None of these

62. Calcite, Dolomite and Hornblendes are the ... minerals-
(a) Calcium (b) Sulphur
(c) Potassium (d) None of these

63. The earth mainly consists of
(a) Three spheres (b) Four spheres
(c) Five spheres (d) All the above

64. The earth's element crust is a partly of
(a) Lithosphere (b) Atmosphere
(c) Hydrosphere (d) All the above

65. The soil column includes
(a) A horizon (b) B-horizon
(c) A & B - horizon (d) None of the above

66. The lithosphere is mainly made up of
(a) Igneous rocks (b) Sedimentary rocks
(c) Metamorphic rocks (d) All the above

67. Igneous rocks are formed by
(a) Weathering of sedimentary rocks
(b) Cooling of molten magma
(c) Metamorphic or sedimentary rocks
(d) None of the above

68. Total weightt is contributed by different spheres as
(a) 93.06% lithosphere, 6.91% hydrosphere 0.03% atmosphere
(b) 92.03% lithosphere, 7.01% hydrosphere 0.96% atmosphere
(c) 6.91% lithosphere 93.06 hydrosphere 0.03% atmosphere
(d) None of the above

69. The most abundant mineral present in the earth's crust is
(a) Quartz (b) Hornblende
(c) Feldspar (d) Mica

70. The mineral gypsum has chemical composition
(a) $CaSO_4$ (b) $CaSO_4.2H_2O$
(c) $CaSO_4.5H_2O$ (d) None of these

71. The mineral limonite has chemical composition
(a) Fe_2O_3 (b) $Fe_2O_{3.}3H_2O$
(c) Fe_3O_4 (d) None of these

72. Most resistant mineral present in soil is
    (a) Mica (b) Hornblende
    (c) Quartz (d) None of these
73. Chlorite and Hornblendes are the minerals
    (a) Mg (b) K.
    (c) p (d) Na
74. The agricultural wealth collects largest share from
    (a) Alluvial soil (b) Red soil
    (c) Black soil (d) Laterite soil
75. The clay fraction of the red soils in rich is
    (a) Basalt (b) Kaolinite
    (c) Gypsum (d) All of the above
76. The land capacity classes are based on the
    (a) Cultivation
    (b) Grazing
    (c) Forestry
    (d) The intensity of hazards and the limitations of use
77. Yellow colour belonging to class it is suitable for
    (a) Raising pastures
    (b) Growing cultivated crops
    (c) Forests and wild life food and covered
    (d) All of these
78. The area of alluvial soils in India is
    (a) 75 mha (b) 250 sq.km
    (c) 110 sq. km (d) 120 mha
79. Alluvial soils are found mostly in
    (a) Kerala, Karnataka and Maharashtra
    (b) A.P., M.P. and Assam
    (c) U.P., Punjab, Haryana, Bihar and W.B.
    (d) None of the above
80. Alluvial soils are rich in
    (a) Fe, Al (b) K_2O, P_2O_5 and lime
    (c) Nitrogen (d) Si, Cu
81. Desert soils are found in
    (a) Arid and humid region (b) Humid and sub-humid region
    (c) Arid and semi-arid region (d) All of the above region

82. Total area in India under desert soils is
(a) 18.2 m.ha (b) 24.2 m.ha
(c) 29 m.ha (d) 28.2 m.ha

83. The headquarters of Indian Sol Survey and land Use Organization which was established in 1966 is at
(a) Nagpur (b) New Delhi
(c) Hyderabad (d) Deharadun

84. A well developed soil have
(a) A horizon (b) B horizon
(c) C Horizons (d) All the above

85. Argilic horizon is rich in
(a) Solum (b) Ped
(c) Humus (d) None of the above

86. Which of the following is a mineral horizon
(a) C horizon (b) B horizon
(c) A horizon (d) None of the above

87. Which of the following is a metamorphic rock?
(a) Marble (b) Granite
(c) Biotite (d) Calcite

88. 'Milne' developed the concept of
(a) Soil series (b) Soil consociation
(c) Soil catena (d) Soil association

89. The local name pokkali or cat clays is .... Soil.
(a) Red Soil (b) Peat soil
(c) Black soil (d) Laterite soil

90. Silt material transported by wind are called as
(a) Delta (b) Meander
(c) Loess (d) Aeolin

91. Sand material transported by wind are called as
(a) Delta (b) Meander
(c) Loess (d) Aeolin

92. Five stages of soil development was given by
(a) Mohr and Von Baren (b) Myers
(c) Russel (d) Hillel

93. Age of soil was described by
(a) Jenny (b) Hilgard
(c) Oswall (d) Hillel

94. Area of pedon range from
    (a) 1-2 m^2
    (b) 1-10 m^2
    (c) 1-50 m^2
    (d) 1-100 m^2
95. Zonal concept is given by
    (a) Marbut
    (b) Dokuchaiov
    (c) Oswall
    (d) Hillel
96. Honey- comb structure is diagnostic feature of
    (a) Laterite soil
    (b) Red soil
    (c) Alluvial soil
    (d) Black soil
97. Gilgai-microrelief is diagnostic feature of
    (a) Laterite soil
    (b) Red soil
    (c) Alluvial soil
    (d) Black soil
98. Father of Indian soil science
    (a) Marbut
    (b) N.S.Randhwa
    (c) J.W.Leather
    (d) Liebig
99. What is Specific gravity of light mineral?
    (a) Above 2.85 g/cm^3
    (b) Above 1.85 g/cm^3
    (c) Above 23.85 g/cm^3
    (d) Above 4.85 g/cm^3
100. What is Specific gravity of Heavy mineral?
    (a) Below 2.85 g/cm^3
    (b) Below 1.85 g/cm^3
    (c) Below 3.85 g/cm^3
    (d) Below 4.85 g/cm^3
101. Stability index of mineral is given by
    (a) Marbut
    (b) N.S.Randhwa
    (c) Jackson
    (d) Jenny
102. The concept of 'soil as a nutrient bin'
    (a) Marbut
    (b) N.S. Randhwa
    (c) Whitney
    (d) Jenny
103. The atmosphere contain CO_2...........%
    (a) 0.033
    (b) 0.123
    (c) 0.333
    (d) 1.20
104. What is density of earth crust
    (a) 9.0 to 12.0 g/cm^3
    (b) 2.6 to 3.0 g/cm^3
    (c) 2.6 to 4.0 g/cm^3
    (d) 3.0 to 4.5 g/cm^3
105. What is density of Mantle
    (a) 3.0 to 4.5 g/cm^3
    (b) 2.6 to 3.0 g/cm^3
    (c) 2.6 to 4.0 g/cm^3
    (d) 1.6 to 3.0 g/cm^3

106. What is density of Core
(a) 3.0 to 4.5 g/cm^3 (b) 9.0 to 12.0 g/cm^3
(c) 2.6 to 4.0 g/cm^3 (d) 1.6 to 3.0 g/cm^3

107. What is density of common rocks
(a) 3.0 to 4.5 g/cm^3 (b) 9.0 to 12.0 g/cm^3
(c) 2.6 to 2.7 g/cm^3 (d) 1.6 to 3.0 g/cm^3

108. What is the thickness of mantle
(a) 2900 km (b) 3500 km
(c) 1100 km (d) 2100 km

109. What is the thickness of core
(a) 2900 km (b) 3500 km
(c) 1100 km (d) 2100 km

110. Earth core contains high proportions of
(a) Fe (b) Ni
(c) Both a and b (d) Mn

111. Percentage of Aluminum in the earth crust.......%
(a) 46.6 (b) 27.72
(c) 8.13 (d) 5.00

112. Percentage of iron in the earth crust.......%
(a) 46.6 (b) 27.72
(c) 8.13 (d) 5.00

113. Percentage of oxygenin the earth crust.......%
(a) 46.6 (b) 27.72
(c) 8.13 (d) 5.00

114. Percentage of Aluminum in the earth crust.......%
(a) 46.6 (b) 27.72
(c) 8.13 (d) 5.00

115. These two element are found in ¾ of the earth crust
(a) Oxygen and Silicon (b) Silicon and Iron
(c) Oxygen and Calcium (d) Oxygen and Sodium

116. Out of 106 element, ...element are sufficiently abundant in earth crust
(a) 52 (b) 24
(c) 12 (d) 8

117. These rocks are contributed 74% in upper 5 km earth crust
(a) Igneous rocks (b) Sedimentary rocks
(c) Metamorphic rocks (d) None of these

118. These rocks are contributed 18% in upper 5 km earth crust
   (a) Igneous rocks (b) Sedimentary rocks
   (c) Metamorphic rocks (d) None of these
119. What is the percentage of shales in upper 5 km earth crust
   (a) 8% (b) 15%
   (c) 7% (d) 52%
120. What is the percentage of sandstone in upper 5 km earth crust
   (a) 8% (b) 15%
   (c) 7% (d) 52%
121. What is the percentage of Granite in upper 5 km earth crust
   (a) 8% (b) 15%
   (c) 7% (d) 52%
122. What is the percentage of Basalt in upper 5 km earth crust
   (a) 3%. (b) 15%
   (c) 7% (d) 52%
123. What is the percentage of Limestone and dolomite in upper 5 km earth crust
   (a) 8% (b) 15%
   (c) 7% (d) 52%
124. A naturally occurring, homogenous element that has a definite chemical composition is called
   (a) Rocks (b) Minerals
   (c) Gravel (d) Peat soil
125. Example of non crystalline mineral
   (a) Allophane (b) chalcedony
   (c) Both a and b (d) None of these
126. Olivine have hardness on mho scale
   (a) 6.5-7.0 (b) 5.0-6.0
   (c) 2.0-2.5 (d) 6.0-6.5
127. Pyroxne and ambhibole have hardness on mho scale
   (a) 6.5-7.0 (b) 5.0-6.0
   (c) 2.0-2.5 (d) 6.0-6.5
128. Biotite and Muscovite have hardness on mho scale
   (a) 6.5-7.0 (b) 5.0-6.0
   (c) 2.0-2.5 (d) 6.0-6.5
129. Anorthite and Orthoclase have hardness on mho scale
   (a) 6.5-7.0 (b) 5.0-6.0
   (c) 2.0-2.5 (d) 6.0-6.5

130. One of the most mineral found in sand and silt fraction of soil
(a) Quartz (b) Feldspars
(c) Pyroxene (d) Olivine

131. In India, the area under red soils is:
(a) 8.0 m ha. (b) 5.1 m. ha
(c) 7.5 mha (d) 0.5 mha

132. Red soil are found maximum in
(a) M.P. (b) Assam
(c) U.P. (d) Tamul Nadu

133. Horizontal layers in the soil profile are referred to as: J
(a) Horizontal zones (b) Rhizonsphoeres
(c) Soil horizon (d) Soil columns

134. Climatic factors e.g., temperature and moisture help in process of soil formation by
(a) Influencing microbial activity and chemical reactions
(b) Melting bed rock
(c) Changing parent material
(d) Changing soil particle size

135. Soils are surveyed and classified on the basis of the distinctive characteristics of
(a) Soil column (b) Soil sample
(c) Soil horizon (d) Parent materials

136. A branch of science that deals with the study of origin of the soil, its classification and its description is known as
(a) Pedology (b) Ecology
(c) Edaphology (d) Geology

137. Decomposition of organic matter. cycling of nutrient including addition of nitrogen, which are vitally important process in soil formation are made possible by present of:
(a) Soil pH (b) Soil minerals
(c) Soil colloids (d) Soil microbes

138. Soil is biochemically withered part of
(a) Parent material (b) Organic matter
(c) Regolith (d) Bedrock

139. A mass of unconsolidated debris varying in composition from place to place and covering bedrock is defined as:
(a) Soil horizon (b) Soil debris
(c) Regolith (d) Soil profile

140. Quartzite are metamorphic rocks derived from:
(a) Slate (b) Granite
(c) Limestone (d) Quartz
141. Alluvial soils in India are
(a) Very rare (b) Most extensive soils
(c) Found desert (d) Least fertile
142. The area of black soil in India is
(a) 5.46 m. ha (b) 75.0 m.ha
(c) 54.6 m ha (d) 28.5 m. ha
143. Black soil in the largest group of Indian soils
(a) First (b) Second
(c) Third (d) None of these
144. Which of the following state has maximum black soils
(a) Haryana (b) Bihar
(c) Maharashtra (d) U.P.
145. Black soils are .... when wet and very hard when dry
(a) Hard (b) Very soft
(c) Very hard (d) Soft
146. Soil horizon A′ E and B′ together is called as
(a) Soil solum (b) Epipedons
(c) Soil profile (d) None of these
147. Black soils have ... amount of lime and P
(a) High (b) Low
(c) Very high (d) Very low
148. The contribution of Hill soils in India is about
(a) 4.5 m ha (b) 2.8 m ha
(c) 1.3 m.ha (d) 10.0 mha
149. Which of the following is not a igneous rocks?
(a) Granite (b) Dibase
(c) Marble (d) Quartzite
150. Which of the following is an igneous rock?
(a) Quartz (b) Mica schist
(c) Marble (d) Slate
151. In detailed soil survey the base maps used having scale.
(a) 1″-1 mile (b) 1″-8 mile
(c) 1″-16 mile (d) None of these

152. The new comprehensive soil classification is based on:
    (a) Physical and chemical properties of soil
    (b) Genetic characters
    (c) a and b both
    (d) None of the above
153. 'A' Horizon of the soil is also designated as
    (a) Eluviated horizon (b) a and c both
    (c) Illuviated horizon (d) None of the above
154. Change in texture and mineral composition of igneous and sedimentary rocks by the action of intense heat and high pressure result in the formation of
    (a) Compact tocks (b) Resistant rocks
    (c) Metamorphic rocks (d) Decomposable rocks
155. About 30-90 per cent absorption power of mineral
    (a) Organic matter (b) Soil microflora
    (c) Growing crops (d) Soil fauna
156. Slates are metamorphic rocks derived from
    (a) Limestone (b) Shales
    (c) Basalt (d) Granite
157. Rocks form which the soils develop are called
    (a) Parent soils (b) Soil materials
    (c) Parent material (d) Primitive soils
158. Conglomerate, sandstone shale and lime stone are
    (a) Metamorphic rocks (b) Igneous rocks
    (c) Sedimentary rocks (d) Morphogenic rocks
159. Saline soils occur mostly in
    (a) Punjab (b) Jammu and Kashmir
    (c) Madhva Pradesh (d) Haryana
160. Gnesis in metamorphic rocks derived from
    (a) Granite (b) Slate
    (c) Limestone (d) Quartz
161. The Chemical decomposition of rocks is brought about by
    (a) Solution and Hydrolysis (b) Oxdation and Reduction
    (c) Carbonation (d) All the above
162. The common sedimentary rocks are
    (a) Conglomerate (b) Shale and limestone
    (c) Sandstone (d) All of the these

163. Unconsolidated sedimentary rocks are the forms
    (a) Alluvial deposits
    (b) Glacial deposits
    (c) Aeolian deposits
    (d) All of the above
164. The principal agents of physical weathering are
    (a) Temperature
    (b) Plants
    (c) Wind and water
    (d) All of the above
165. How many kinds of main rocks are there?
    (a) 2
    (b) 3
    (c) 1
    (d) 4
166. The components of soil are
    (a) Mineral material
    (b) Water and air
    (c) Organic matter
    (d) All of these
167. Igneous rocks are formed by the
    (a) Cooling, hardening and crystallizing of various kinds of lavas
    (b) Action of intense heart and high pressure or both resulting in considerable change in the texture and mineral composition
    (c) Weathering
    (d) Consolidation of fragmentary rock materials and the products of their decomposition by water
168. The common igneous rocks found in India are
    (a) Basalts of the deccan trap (Basic)
    (b) Granites (acidic)
    (c) None of the above
    (d) Both a and b
169. A modern system of Soil Taxonomy was developed by
    (a) The International System
    (b) The USDA
    (c) The All India Workshop held in 1969
    (d) None of the above
170. On the basis of total mass, the relative abundance of the given elements in the earths crustus such that
    (a) O_2Si Fe Al
    (b) O_2 Al Si Fe
    (c) O_2 Si Al Fe
    (d) Si O_2 Fe Al
171. The ancient crystalline and metamorphic rocs on meteoric weathering have given rise to
    (a) Alluvial soil
    (b) Cotton soil
    (c) Red soil
    (d) None of the above
172. The unconsolidated material in the underlying rock is called
    (a) Earth
    (b) Soil
    (c) Regolith
    (d) Solum

173. Which one of the following minerals is least weatherable in soil?
(a) Olivine (b) Quartz
(c) Biotite (d) Calcite

174. According to traditional nomenclature, the order(s) of the alluvial soil are
(a) Entisol (b) Alfisol
(c) Inceptisol (d) All of the above

175. Smallest unit of soil classification is
(a) Grade groups (b) Order
(c) Series (d) Sub-group

176. The soil which is comparable with the chernozenis of Russia and the praine soils of the cotton growing states of the cotton growing states of the USA especially the black adobe of California
(a) Alluvial soil (b) Red soil
(c) Black soil (d) Laterite soil

177. There can actually be a build up of toxic concentrations of Fe^{2+} in the soil solution of...
(a) Aridsol (b) Latosol
(c) Histosol (d) Vertisol

178. Silicon is the most abundant element in the earth crust
(a) Third (b) Sixth
(c) Second (d) Fourth

179. Properties of the silicon deficient Hqaian Soils include
(a) High base saturation (b) High total silicon
(c) High pH (d) High total aluminium content

180. It is generally accepted that the Gramineae members contain times the silicon concentration normally found in legumes and other dicotyledonous plants
(a) 10-20 (b) 20-30
(c) 05-10 (d) 30-40

181. Pedology considers soil as a
(a) Natural body
(b) Medium for plant growth
(c) Powdered rock mass of the earth's crust
(d) Purely a synthesized one

182. The layers in soil are referred to as
(a) Hard pans (b) Horizons
(c) Profile (d) Pedocals

183. Soils high in swelling clays which crack widely upon drying resulting in shrinking, shearing and soil mass movement are characteristics of
(a) Podzols (b) Entisols
(c) Ultisols (d) Vertisols
184. Which state is devoid of arid zone?
(a) Madhya Pradesh (b) Andhra Pradesh
(c) Punjab (d) Maharashtra
185. Indian Institute of Soil Science is located at
(a) Ludhiana (b) Hisar
(c) New Delhi (d) Bhopal
186. The layer in the soil profile where material removed from the two overlying horizons is deposited is called
(a) A-Horizon (b) D-horizons
(c) C-horizon (d) B-horizon
187. Chemical weathering is governs mostly by the process
(a) Hydrogen (b) Hydrolysis
(c) Carbonation (d) All of these
188. The systematic examination, description, classification and mapping of soil of an area is known as –
(a) Soil survey (b) Soil classification
(c) Soil mapping (d) All of the above
189. All India Soil Survey and Land Use Organization was established n –
(a) 1962 (b) 1050
(c) 1956 (d) 1960
190. The head office of All India Soil Survey and Land Use Organization is at –
(a) Madras (b) Bombay
(c) Nagpur (d) New Delhi
191. The diagnostic horizon in Alfisol is termed
(a) Spodic (b) Oxic
(c) Argillic (d) Mollic
192. The equation of soil formation, S=f (Cl, o, r, p, t) was given by
(a) Glinka (b) Jenny
(c) Kellog (d) Dokuchaev
193. Which of the following is not a metamorphic rock
(a) Gneiss (b) Sandostone
(c) Limestone (d) Conglomerate
194. Which of the following is not a sedimentary rock
(a) Limestone (b) Sandostone
(c) Conglomerate (d) Gneiss

195. The soil layer of maximum leaching is indicated by the symbol
(a) A_1 (b) A_2
(c) B (d) 82

196. The horizons which make up the profile of a lowest soil would include
(a) A, C, & O (b) A, B, C & O
(c) A, B & C (d) B & O

197. A combination of many taxonomic unit likes oil series, phase or types is called-
(a) Soil series (b) Soil complex
(c) Soil variant (d) Soil association

198. The patterns of occurrence of various soil taxonomic units on the detailed map is called-
(a) Soil phase (b) Soil association
(c) Soil variant (d) Soil complex

199. The texture of surface soil of surface horizon is called
(a) Soil phase (b) Soil variant
(c) Soil series (d) Soil type

200. The characteristics of surface soil which have important bearing in soil management and crop production. is known as
(a) Soil phase (b) Soil series
(c) Soil variant (d) None of these

201. The representation of surface feature on mp and heir identification, is called
(a) Soil variant (b) Soil map
(c) Soil legend (d) None of these

202. An abrupt change in texture class of no continuity found between B and C horizon, is termed as
(a) Lithological discontinuity (b) Regolith discontinuity
(c) Textural change (d) N Tone of the above

203. Example of cumulous material are
(a) Gneiss (b) Till plain
(c) Peat and Muck (d) Colluvial

204. Aeoline deposits are formed by the transportation of materials through
(a) Wind (b) Sea
(c) Running water (d) Ice

205. Solum is made up of
(a) C horizon (b) 'C+D' horizon
(c) 'A+B' horizon (d) 'C; horizon

206. Identify which of the following is a passive soil forming factors
    (a) Relief (b) Climate
    (c) Biosphere (d) None of the these
207. Aridisol soils are found in the region of
    (a) Humid (b) Submerged
    (c) Arid (d) None of these
208. The dominant colour of spectral (rainbow) in soil indicates
    (a) Kaoline type of clay mineral (b) Value
    (c) Hue (d) Chroma
209. Soils formed under impeded drainage condition where movement of air and water is restricted is known as
    (a) Acid soil (b) Podzol
    (c) Gley Soil (d) Cherozem
210. Physical weathering causes
    (a) Alternation of rocks and minerals
    (b) Decomposition of rocks and minerals
    (c) Disintegration of rocks and minerals
    (d) Synthesis of rocks and minerals
211. Consider the following statements regardmg the causes of low crop productivity of sandy soils:
    (1) Sandy soils have very low water retention capacity
    (2) Applied plant nutrients easily leach out through drainage
    (3) Sandy soils have very low organic matter content.
    (4) Sandy soil easily fix applied P. of these statements –
    (a) 1, 2 & 3 are correct (b) 2, 3 & 4 are correct
    (c) 1, 2 & 4 are correct (d) 1, 3, & 4 correct
212. Percentage of soil solids in soil is
    (a) 50% (b) 40%
    (c) 30% (d) 60%
213. Which of the following is known as father of pedology
    (a) V.V. Dokuchaiev (b) D.G. Vilensky
    (c) K.D. Glinka (d) C.F. Marbut
214. The average arable surface soiL may be considered to have a particle density of about
    (a) 3.00 gms/cc (b) 2.64 gms/cc
    (c) 2.70 gms/cc (d) 3.00 gms/cc
215. The illuviation is zone of
    (a) Hard crust (b) Leaching
    (c) Accumulation (d) None of these

216. The maximum moisture is available to plant at
(a) Wilting point (b) Hygroscopic coefficient
(c) Saturation (d) Field capacity

217. The method of survey adopted or intensive cultivation is
(a) Detailed survey
(b) Reonnaissance survey
(c) Detailed and reconnaissance survey
(d) All of the above

218. Soil air contain
(a) 2.5% CO_2 (b) 0.02% CO_2
(c) 3.0% CO_2 (d) 0.25% CO_2

219. The diagnostic surface horizons are called
(a) Polypedon (b) Pedon
(c) Epipedon (d) All of them

220. A thick dark coloured horizon which have high base saturation (50% or more) high organic malter content and with strong soil-structure, is called
(a) Ochric epipedon (b) Histic epipedon
(c) Umbric epipedon (d) Mollic epipiedon

221. An epipedon which has dark colour low in base saturation is called
(a) Ochric epipedon (b) Umbric epipedon
(c) Histric epipedon (d) Mollic epipiedon

222. A man made epipedon which is similar to mo lic epipedon in many characters expect P_20_5 content (more than 250 ppm) is
(a) Umbric epipedon (b) Anthtropic epipedon
(c) Ochric epipedon (d) Hstic epipedon

223. In India. the area under red soils is
(a) 8.0 m. ha (b) 5.1 m.ha
(c) 7.5 m. ha (d) 10.5 m.ha

224. Red soil are found maximum in
(a) M.P. (b) Assam
(c) U.P. (d) Tamil Nadu

225. Horizontal layers in the soil profile are referred to as
(a) Horizontal zones (b) Rhizonsphoeres
(c) Soil horizon (d) Soil columns

226. Ammonia is transformed into nitrste by
(a) Fungi (b) Algae
(c) Bacteria (d) Actinomycetes

227. Development of acidity in soil, which is encouraged by humid climate is delayed by

(a) Dolomine is soil | (b) Iron in soil
(c) Earthworms in soil | (d) Lime stone in soil

228. Soil conservation measures are being undertaken in the catchments areas of river valley projects in order to

(a) Check premature siltation of reservoirs
(b) Increase the rainfall in the catchments areas
(c) Increase the area under forests
(d) Provide employment to displaced persons

229. Climatic factors e.g., temperature and moisture help in process of soil formation by

(a) Influencing microbial activity and chemical reactions
(b) Melting bed rock
(c) Changing parent material
(d) Changing soil particle size

230. Soils are surveyed and classified on the basis of the distinctive characteristics of

(a) Soil column | (b) Soil sample
(c) Soil horizon | (d) Parent materials

231. A branch of science that deals with the stud of origin of the soil. its classification and its description is known as

(a) Pedology | (b) Ecology
(c) Edapholog | (d) Geology

232. The area of black soil in India is

(a) 5.46 m. ha | (b) 75.0 m. ha
(c) 54.6 m. ha | (d) 28,5 m. ha

233. Black soil in the largest group of Indian soils.

(a) First | (b) Second
(c) Third | (d) None of these

234. Which of the following state has maximum black soils

(a) Haryana | (b) Bihar
(c) Maharashtra | (d) U.P.

235. Black soils are .... when wet and very hard when dry

(a) Hard | (b) Very soil
(c) Very hard | (d) Soft

236. Soil horizon A′ E and B together is called as

(a) Soil soluni | (b) Epipedons
(c) Soil profile | (d) None of these

237. Black soils have ... amount of lime and P

(a) High (b) Low
(c) Very high (d) Very low

238. The contribution of Hill soils in India is about

(a) 4.5 m ha (b) 2.8 m ha
(c) 1.3 m.ha (d) 10.0 mha

239. Which of the following element is mobile m soil?

(a) N (b) Mg
(c) K (d) Ca

240. 95 to 99, 5% portion of plant tissues are made up of

(a) N.P and K (b) Ca, Mg and C
(c) C, H. and O (d) None of these

241. If the particle size is 2 mm to 7.5 cm than it is known as

(a) Silt (b) Stones
(c) Gravels (d) Sand

242. Which of the following primary minerals has no good and nutrient holding capacity

(a) Feldspar (b) Mica
(c) Quartz (d) All of these

243. Lithosphere has about igneous rocks

(a) 75% (b) 95%
(c) 80% (d) 72%

244. Which one of the following sets of soil conditions is more suitable for plant growth?

(a) Sandy soils with high aeration and low water holding capacity.
(b) Clay soils with high water holding capacity and low aeration.
(c) Organic soils with high water holding capacity and low aeration
(d) Loamy soils with medium aeration and medium water holding capacity

245. Which of the following is not a igneous rocks?

(a) Granite (b) Dibase
(c) Marble (d) Quartzite

246. Which of the following is an igneous rock?

(a) 1″-1 mile (b) 1″-8 mile
(c) 1″-16 mile (d) None of these

247. 'A' horizon of the soil is also designated as

(a) Eluviated horizon (b) a and c both
(c) Illuviated horizon (d) None of the above

248. Which of the following is not a metamorphic work ?
    (a) Marble (b) Conglomerate schists
    (c) Quartzite (d) Sand stone
249. Terai soils are deficient in
    (a) Zinc (b) Nitrogen
    (c) Sulphur (d) Phosphorus
250. Change in texture and mineral composition of igneous and sedimentary rocks by the action of intense heat and high pressure result in the formation of
    (a) Compact tocks (b) Resistant rocks
    (c) Metamorphic rocks (d) Decomposable rocks
251. About 30-90 per cent absorption power of mineral soils is on account of
    (a) Organic matter (b) Soil microflora
    (c) Growing crops (d) Soil fauna
252. Slates are metamorphic rocks derived from
    (a) Limestone (b) Shales
    (c) Basait (d) Granite
253. Soils containing high proportion of organic matter have the following colour
    (a) Dark colour (b) Red colour
    (c) Yellow colour (d) Light colour
254. Conglomerate, sandstone shale and lime stone are
    (a) Metamorphic rocks (b) Igneous rocks
    (c) Sedimentary rocks (d) Morphogenic rocks
255. Gneiss in metamorphic rocks derived from
    (a) Granite (b) Slate
    (c) Limestone (d) Quartz
256. The chemical decomposition of rocks is brought about by
    (a) Solution and Hydrolysis (b) Oxidation and Reduction
    (c) Carbonation (d) All the above
257. The common sedimentary rocks are
    (a) Conglomerate (b) Shale and limestone
    (c) Sandstone (d) All of the these
258. Unconsolidated sedimentary rocks are the forms of
    (a) Alluvial deposits (b) Glacial deposits
    (c) Aeolian deposits (d) All of the above
259. The principal agents of physical weathering are
    (a) Temperature (b) Plants
    (c) Wind and water (d) All of the above

260. How many kinds of main rocks are there?
(a) 2 (b) 3
(c) 1 (d) 4
261. The components of soil are
(a) Mineral material (b) Water and air
(c) Organic matter (d) All of these
262. Igneous rocks are formed by the
(a) Cooling, hardening and crystallizing of various kinds of lavas
(b) Action of intense heat and high pressure or both resulting in considerable change in he texture and mineral composition
(c) Weathering
(d) Consolidation of fragmentary rock materials and the products of their decomposition by water
263. The common igneous rocks found in India are
(a) Basalts of the deccan trap (basic)
(b) Granites (acidic)
(c) None of the above
(d) Both a and b
264. The CEC value of illite is ... me/100 g
(a) 10-30 (b) 10-20
(c) 10-40 (d) 20-30
265. The CEC value of kaolinite is ... me/100 g.
(a) 3-10 (b) 80-150
(c) 10-30 (d) None of these

ANSWERS

1(a) 2(a) 3(a) 4(b) 5(d) 6(d) 7(a) 8(c) 9(d) 10(b) 11(c) 12(a) 13(c) 14(b) 15(a) 16(a) 17(d) 18(d) 19(c) 20(b) 21(c) 22(a) 23(a) 24(c) 25(c) 26(c) 27(b) 28(b) 29(c) 30(c) 31(c) 32(a) 33(b) 34(b) 35(c) 36(d) 37(d) 38(d) 39(b) 40(a) 41(a) 42(d) 43(c) 44(d) 45(a) 46(a) 47(d) 48(d) 49(c) 50(d) 51(a) 52(d) 53(a) 54(c) 55(a) 56(c) 57(c) 58(a) 59(b) 60(b) 61(c) 62(a) 63(a) 64(a) 65(c) 66(a) 67(b) 68(a) 69(c) 70(b) 71(b) 72(c) 73(a) 74(a) 75(b) 76(d) 77(d) 78(a) 79(c) 80(b) 81(c) 82(c) 83(b) 84(d) 85(a) 86(c) 87(a) 88(c) 89(d) 90(c) 91(d) 92(a) 93(a) 94(b) 95(b) 96(a) 97(d) 98(c) 99(a) 100(a) 101(c) 102(c) 103(a) 104(b) 105(a) 106(b) 107(c) 108(a) 109(b) 110(c) 111(c) 112(d) 113(a) 114(b) 115(a) 116(d) 117(b) 118(a) 119(d) 120(b) 121(b) 122(a) 123(c) 124(b) 125(c) 126(a) 127(b) 128(c) 129(d) 130(a) 131(b) 132(d) 133(c) 134(a) 135(d) 136(a) 137(d) 138(c) 139(c) 140(d) 141(b) 142(a) 143(b) 144(c) 145(d) 146(a) 147(a) 148(c) 149(d)

150(a) 151(a) 152(a) 153(a) 154(c) 155(a) 156(b) 157(c) 158(c) 159(d)
160(a) 161(d) 162(d) 163(d) 164(d) 165(b) 166(d) 167(a) 168(d) 169(b)
170(c) 171(c) 172(c) 173(b) 174(d) 175(c) 176(c) 177(b) 178(c) 179(d)
180(a) 181(a) 182(b) 183(d) 184(a) 185(d) 186(b) 187(d) 188(a) 189(c)
190(c) 191(c) 192(b) 193(d) 194(d) 195(b) 196(b) 197(d) 198(d) 199(d)
200(a) 201(c) 202(a) 203(c) 204(a) 205(c) 206(a) 207(c) 208(c) 209(c)
210(c) 211(a) 212(a) 213(a) 214(b) 215(c) 216(d) 217(a) 218(b) 219(c)
220(d) 221(b) 222(b) 223(b) 224(d) 225(c) 226(c) 227(d) 228(a) 229(a)
230(d) 231(a) 232(a) 233(b) 234(c) 235(d) 236(a) 237(a) 238(c) 239(a)
240(c) 241(c) 242(c) 243(b) 244(d) 245(d) 246(a) 247(a) 248(d) 249(a)
250(c) 251(c) 252(b) 253(a) 254(c) 255(a) 256(d) 257(d) 258(d) 259(d)
260(b) 261(d) 262(a) 263(d) 264(c) 265(a)

CHAPTER - 4

Soil Fertility and Fertilizers

1. All India Coordinated Project on Long Term Fertilizer Experiments (LTFE) was started in
   (a) 1970 (b) 1975
   (c) 1980 (d) 1985
2. Critical limit based fertilizer recommendation is useful in recommending
   (a) Primary nutrients (b) Secondary nutrients
   (c) Micro nutrients (d) All of these
3. Soil test crop response (STCR) approach was established by
   (a) Ramamurthy and associates (b) Liebig
   (c) Mitscherlitch (d) None of these
4. In Mitscherlitch - Bray equation, A is referred to
   (a) Maximum possible yield (b) Percentage of maximum yield
   (c) Both a and b (d) None of these
5. Sackette and Stewart technique of nutrient deficiency test is used for nutrients
   (a) K (b) P
   (c) Both a and b (d) Fe
6. Pahala blight of Sugarcane is due the deficiency of
   (a) Fe (b) Mn
   (c) Zn (d) Mo
7. Element responsible for pollen development is
   (a) B (b) Mo
   (c) N (d) P
8. Diagnosis and recommendation integrated system (DRIS) concept was proposed by
   (a) Gilbert (b) Naidu *et al.*
   (c) Beaufils (d) Krishnamoorthy

9. Crop logging concept was defined by
   (a) Reinganum (b) Henry F. Clement
   (c) Liebig (d) Blakman
10. The Book 'Manures and Fertilizers' was written by
   (a) Alexander (b) Tisdale and nelson
   (c) J.S. Kanwar (d) Yawalkar
11. Indian society of Soil Science is established in
   (a) 1934 (b) 1936
   (c) 1980 (d) 1951
12. Essentiality of chlorine for plants was given by
   (a) Nicholas (b) Broyer *et al.*
   (c) E.Gris (d) Springle
13. Which one is considered as organic fertilizer?
   (a) FYM (b) Urea
   (c) Ammonium sulphate (d) DAP
14. The process by which ions are taken into plant roots
   (a) Oasis (b) Absorption
   (c) Advection (d) Adsorption
15. A by product of coastal salt industry- schoenite is a rich source of plant nutrient
   (a) N (b) P
   (c) K (d) Zn
16. The C: N ratio of the soil are fairly constant between
   (a) 10 : 1 to 12 : 1 (b) 50 : 1 to 60 : 1
   (c) 1 : 10 to 1 : 12 (d) 1 : 10 to 12.6
17. Conversion factor for P to P_2O_5 is
   (a) 2.00 (b) 2.5
   (c) 2.29 (d) 1.92
18. The essentiality of N was established by
   (a) E. Gris (b) De Saussure
   (c) Arnon (d) Lip man
19. Soil productivity is basically a:
   (a) Social concept (b) Economic concept
   (c) Physical concept (d) Chemical concept
20. kg/ha=ppm ×_____
   (a) 1.24 (b) 4.48
   (c) 1.12 (d) 2.24

21. The pH value varies from
    (a) 7.00 to 14.00 (b) 0.00 to 7.00
    (c) 0.00 to 14.00 (d) None of these
22. The green manure crop is turned into soil at the stage of crop
    (a) Germination (b) Harvest
    (c) Flowering (d) Boot stage
23. Requirement of phosphorus by the crop is maximum at ____ growth stage
    (a) Initial (b) Flowering
    (e) Lateral (d) Harvest
24. Paddy crop absorbs nitrogen in from of
    (a) NH_2 (b) NH_4
    (c) NO_3 (c) N_2
25. Organic nitrogen converted in to NH_4 from is known as
    (a) Nitrification (b) Ammonification
    (c) Dentrification (d) Immoblization
26. The nutrient required for quality maintenance in potato
    (a) Zinc (b) Phosphours
    (c) Iron (d) Potassium
27. The water in soil is called
    (a) Humus (b) Porous
    (c) Biomass (d) Soil solution
28. Who postulated the law of the minimum?
    (a) Joseph priestly (b) Theodore de Saussure
    (c) Justus von Liebig (d) Machu Picchu
29. The most common land use in the United States is
    (a) Urban (b) Forest
    (c) Pasture (d) Crops
30. How many chemical elements are generally recognized as essential for plant growth?
    (a) 17 (b) 12
    (c) 34 (d) 8
31. In general, which people are most healthy?
    (a) Malnourished (b) Adequately fed
    (c) Over nourished (d) No general pattern exists
32. On an annual basis, which does the world produce on greatest tonnage?
    (a) Grain (b) Poultry
    (c) Beef (d) People

33. According to United Nations FAO forecasts, how will the amount of arable land per person worldwide change between 2000 and 2050?
    (a) It will decline more than 20% (b) It will decline less than 20%
    (c) It will remain steady (d) It will increase slightly
34. Which practice adversely affects the soil?
    (a) Leaving the soil bare
    (b) Driving vehicles over the soil
    (c) Using heavy fosse of ammonium fertilizer
    (d) All the above
35. Which plant nutrient most often controls the rate of organic matter decomposition?
    (a) Nitrogen (b) Phosphorus
    (c) Potassium (d) Zinc
36. The contents of organic matter would normally include about how much carbon?
    (a) 90% (b) 50%
    (c) 10% (d) 0.1%
37. Long chains of sugar molecules that help cement soil aggregates are
    (a) Amines (b) Chromatin
    (c) Polysaccharides (d) Enzymes
38. Which of the following is an essential element for plants?
    (a) Helium (b) Silver
    (c) Selenium (d) Copper
39. Which essential element is obtained from air and water?
    (a) Carbon (b) Oxygen
    (c) Hydrogen (d) All the above
40. Which of the following implies a loss of nitrogen from the soil?
    (a) Mineralization (b) Nitrification
    (c) Volatilization (d) immobilization
41. Which of the following is a source of soil nitrogen?
    (a) Leaching (b) Denitrification
    (c) Symbiotic nitrogen fixation (d) Immobilization
42. Most potassium used by plants in a given season comes from soluble K and:
    (a) Apatite (b) Fixed K^+
    (c) Exchangeable K^+ (d) Symbiotic K^+
43. Rice and aquatic plants use which form of nitrogen?
    (a) Nitrate (b) Nitrite
    (c) Ammonium (d) Urea

44. What is inhibited by a nitrification inhibitor?
   (a) Conversion of nitrate
   (b) Conversion of ammonium to nitrate
   (c) Conversion of amino acid to ammonium
   (d) Conversion of nitrogen gas
45. Which is a controlled release fertilizer?
   (a) Anhydrous ammonia (b) Ammonium nitrate
   (c) Ammonium sulfate (d) Sulfur coated urea
46. Which of the following elements is typically least abundant in the soil solution?
   (a) Nitrogen (b) Phosphorus
   (c) Potassium (d) Calcium
47. Reacting rock phosphate with sulfuric acid forms which product?
   (a) MAP (b) Sulfur-coated urea
   (c) Triple super phosphate (d) Super phosphate
48. Which element is taken from the air and placed in the soil by microorganisms ?
   (a) Nitrogen (b) Phosphorus
   (c) Potassium (d) All the above
49. Which environmental condition favors denitrification?
   (a) Low nitrate levels (b) Low temperatures
   (c) Low 0_2 levels (d) All the above
50. How many micronutrients are generally recognized as essential to plants?
   (a) 3 (b) 6
   (c) 9 (d) 8
51. How do farmers most commonly apply calcium to soil?
   (a) As liquid fertilizer (b) As a foliar spray
   (c) As a chelate (d) As lime
52. Gypsum contains which two plant nutrients?
   (a) Calcium and sulfur (b) Calcium and sodium
   (c) Phosphorus and iron (d) Sulfur and iron
53. Which of the following might alleviate iron deficiency on a farm ?
   (a) Lower the soil pH
   (b) Grow plants that produce siderophores
   (c) Add chelated iron to the soil
   (d) All the above

54. Which crops are most susceptible to zinc deficiency?
    (a) Forage grasses (b) Deciduous fruit
    (c) Clovers (d) Tomatoes
55. The important enzymes nitrate reductase and nitrogenase contain which micronutrient metal
    (a) Nitrogen (b) Zinc
    (c) Molybdenum (d) Boron
56. Which plants are known to benefit from sodium?
    (a) Fruit trees (b) Turf grasses
    (c) Tropical ornamentals (d) Halophytic desert species
57. What is the main fertilizer used to correct chlorine deficiency?
    (a) Potassium chloride (b) Sodium chloride
    (c) Sulfate chloride (d) Chlorine sulfate
58. Which of the following elements undergoes many microbial reactions and transformations, Similar to those of nitrogen?
    (a) Nickel (b) Sulfur
    (c) Potassium (d) Manganese
59. Which of the following is normally a goal of land managers regarding soil fertility?
    (a) To increase yields
    (b) To reduce cost per unit of production
    (c) To avoid environment
    (d) All the above
60. Which of the elements below are extracted from the soil the greatest quantity by a grain crop such as corn, oats or flee?
    (a) Sulfur (b) Magnesium
    (c) Nitrogen (d) Phosphate
61. The saturated paste extract is typically used to measure
    (a) Soil salinity (b) Soil acidity
    (c) Soil nitrate (d) Soil phosphate
62. Extracting the concentration of which of the following elements is most important in soil resting?
    (a) Nitrogen (b) Phosphorus
    (c) Potassium (d) Sulfur
63. For which element would a deficiency appear as dark as green tissue, stunting, and purple coloring in order leave
    (a) Iron (b) Phosphorus
    (c) Nitrogen (d) Magnesium

64. Which of the following nutrients is least mobile in the plant?
(a) Chlorine (b) Magnesium
(c) Sulfur (d) Boron

65. A farmer needing 50 pounds of nitrogen per acre needs how acre?
(a) 17 (b) 147
(c) 68 (d) None of the above

66. If nitrogen fertilizer is incorporated instead of left on the soil surface, the loss of nitrogen by which of the following processes can be expected to be reduced?
(a) Leaching
(b) Immobilization by clay minerals
(c) Volatilization of nitrate by denitrification
(d) Volatilization of ammonia

67. Which of the following are sources of micronutrients?
(a) Igneous rocks (b) Horse manure
(c) Decomposing soil organic (d) All of the above

68. Which anionic plant micronutrient becomes more available at low pH and is rather easily leached from sandy soils?
(a) Iron (b) Chlorine
(c) Molybdenum (d) Boron

69. Which of the following is (are) important in managing micronutrient fertility in soils?
(a) Control of drainage (b) Liming practices
(c) Choice of crop (d) All of the above

70. A........... on a farm will probably eventually lead to eutrophication problems in nearby surface water
(a) Negative (b) Riparian buffer strip
(c) Positive nutrient balance (d) None of the these

71. "Xenobiotics" are.
(a) Any chemicals that contain carbon
(b) Products used for the biological control
(c) Special soil amendment organic farming
(d) Synthetic organic compounds not found in nature

72. Soil quality is generally enhanced by greater
(a) Organic matter content (b) Stability of soil structure
(c) Abundance of soil microbes (d) All of the above

73. Which of the following indicators of soil quality is (are) sentitive to soil management over periods of just a few years?
    (a) Soil mineral contents (b) Bulk density
    (c) Soil texture (d) Soil depth
74. The plant nutrient when supplied in excess prolongs the growing period and delay crop maturity is
    (a) Phosphorus (b) Nitrogen
    (c) Iron (d) Potassium
75. Molybdenum is a component of
    (a) Chlorophyll (b) Nitrogenase
    (c) Cell wall (d) None of above
76. Zinc deficiency occurs in crops growing in soils having high phosphorus
    (a) Calcareous soils (b) Light soils
    (c) Soils having pH 7.5 (d) Soils low in phosphorus
77. Thc rate of water absorption by plants is decreased due to deficiency of
    (a) Potassium (b) Iron
    (c) Boron (d) Manganese
78. The secondary plant element is
    (a) Nitrogen (b) Zinc
    (c) Boron (d) Calcium
79. Pungency in mustard oil is caused by
    (a) Amino acid (b) Glucosilates
    (c) Erusic acid (d) None of these
80. Which of the following is not a method of fertilizer application by the way of localized placement ?
    (a) Band (b) Deep
    (c) Hill (d) Ring
81. Which of the following is a high salt tolerant crop?
    (a) Moong (b) Urd
    (c) Lucerne (d) Arhar
82. Phosphorus is taken by plants in the form of
    (a) Phosphorus carbonate (b) Phosphorus sulphate
    (c) Phosphoric acid (d) Phosphorus chloride
83. Green revolution in wheat is basically attributed to
    (a) Higher use of N, P, K fertilizers
    (b) Greater availability of irrigation
    (c) Greater use of seeds of high yielding varieties
    (d) Greater use of plant protection chemicals

84. Whiptail in cauliflower is caused due to
(a) Deficiency of boron (b) Deficiency of iron
(c) Deficiency of molybdenum (d) Deficiency of sulphur

85. Urea hydrolysis in the soil produces
(a) Uric acid (b) Ammonium carbonate
(c) Amides (d) Ammonium hydroxide

86. Which of the following is not high salt tolerant crop
(a) Sugarcane (b) Maize
(c) Barley (d) Sugar beat

87. The importance of nitrogen is
(a) To increase growth and green colour in plants
(b) To increase root development
(c) To increase disease resistance
(d) To help in starch formation

88. The succulence and lodging in plants is due to excessive application of
(a) Potash (b) Phosphorus
(c) Nitrogen (d) Zinc

89. Deficiency of several elements is exhibited first in the apical region of the
(a) Autolysis (b) Mobile nature
(c) immobile nature (d) Translocation

90. Phosphorus occurs in soils in
(a) Organic forms only (b) Inorganic forms only
(c) Both inorganic and organic forms (d) None of the above

91. Iron helps in chlorophyll synthesis because
(a) It is absent in chlorophyll
(b) It is associated with chlorophyll
(c) It activate enzyme nitrogen reductase
(d) None of the above

92. Highly available form of phosphorus at pH 7.5 is
(a) $H_2PO_4^-$ (b) $H_2PO_4^{-2}$
(c) PO_3 (d) Inositol

93. Carbon Nitrogen ratio fluctuate widely from 5 to 26, with the average value of around
(a) 04 (b) 14
(c) 24 (d) 34

94. The fertilizer containing nitrogen in amide from is
(a) CAN (b) Ammonium sulphate
(c) Urea (d) Ammonium phosphate

95. Azotobacter is useful in fixing nitrogen from air in
    (a) Non-leguminous crop like rice and wheat
    (b) Soybean
    (c) Leguminous crops
    (d) None of these
96. Which of the following is a micronutrient
    (a) Calcium (b) Zinc
    (c) Phosphorus (d) Nitrogen
97. Deficiency of which of the following element causes general yellowing and poor growth
    (a) Calcium (b) Boron
    (c) Phosphorus (d) Nitrogen
98. In case of ammonia synthesis the reaction is
    (a) Exothermic (b) Endothemic
    (c) Both the above (d) None of these
99. The plants growing following modification for efficient carbon assimilation
    (a) Leaves become broad (b) Stem is modified into thorn
    (c) Leaves become narrower (d) Leaves become leathery
100. Which of the following is commonly used for green manuring in India
    (a) Lentil (b) Pea
    (c) Dhaincha (d) Potato
101. Nitrogenous fertilizers are classified into
    (a) Two group (b) Three group
    (c) Four group (d) None of these
102. Ammonium sulphate contain
    (a) 20% sulphur (b) 24% sulphur
    (c) 16% sulphur (d) 26% sulphur
103. Calcium cynamide contain
    (a) 16 to 28% nitrogen (b) 16 to 18% sulphur
    (c) 16% to 21% sulphur (d) None of the above
104. Sodium nitrate contain
    (a) 18% nitrogen (b) 28% nitrogen
    (c) 16% nitrogen (d) 24% nitrogen
105. In which form phosphorus is absorbed by plants
    (a) PO_4^{3-}, HPO_4^{2-} H_2PO_4 (b) P_2O_5 ions
    (c) Both a and b (d) None of the above

106. The amount of N_2 fixed by clostridiurn is ... Mg N_2 per gin sugar
    (a) 15-25 (b) 7-12
    (c) 25-20 (d) 2-7
107. Which of the following are the slow release fertilizers ?
    (a) Neem cake and super grain urea (b) n-serve
    (c) Surface coated urea (d) All of the above
108. Tricalcium phosphate is soluble in
    (a) Weak acid (b) Strong mineral acid
    (c) None of the above (d) Water
109. Steamed bone meal contain
    (a) 18% P_2O_5 (b) 25% P_2O_5
    (c) 22% P_2O_5 (d) 16% P-$_2O_5$
110. Rock phosphate contains
    (a) 16 to 18% P_2O_5 (b) 20 to 40% P-$_2O_5$
    (c) 20 to 22% P-$_2O_5$ (d) 12 to 16% P-$_2O_5$
111. Single super phosphate (SSP) contains
    (a) 16 to 18% P-$_2O_5$ (b) 20 to 25% P-$_2O_5$
    (c) 20% P-$_2O_5$ (d) 10 to 46% P-$_2O_5$
112. Nutrient index is used to prepare the
    (a) Soil fertility map (b) Soil productivity map
    (c) Both of the above (d) None of the above
113. If nutrient index is less than 1.6, indicates that soil is ... in nutrients
    (a) Average (b) Deficient
    (c) Adequate (d) None of these
114. 1.6 to 2.3 value of nutrient index indicates
    (a) Average fertility of soil (b) Adequate fertility of soil
    (c) Both of the above (d) None of the above
115. The humus myth was effectively deposed by ... by presentation of a paper at a prominent scientific meeting
    (a) Justus Senebier (b) Justus billright
    (c) Jean young (d) Justus von Liebig
116. Rothanisted Agricultural Experiment Station, England was founded by
    (a) J.B. Lawes and J.H. Gilbert (b) Jean Young
    (c) Justus Birliright (d) Justus senebier
117. Some specialists have identified... factors that influence crop growth
    (a) 32 (b) 42
    (c) 52 (d) 22

118. It has been suggested that the ... of sunlight is generally most satisfactory for plant growth
    (a) Halt Spectrum (b) Little more than full spectrum
    (c) Full Spectrum (d) None of these
119. Most effective phosphatic fertilizer for crops in acidic soil is
    (a) DAP (b) SSP
    (c) Rock phosphate (d) None
120. Windbreaks are planted in orchards towards
    (a) South-west (b) North-west
    (c) North-west (d) East-south
121. Pulse crop which does not fix nitrogen from atmosphere easily is
    (a) Arhar (b) Soybean
    (c) Rajma (d) Pea
122. Which of the following elements is not essential elements for plants but proves to be beneficial for some
    (a) Iodine (b) Boron
    (c) Sodium (d) Copper
123. More than 2.3 value of nutrient index indicates
    (a) Adequate fertility of soil
    (b) Adequate productivity of soil
    (c) Average productivity of soil
    (d) None of the above
124. Khaira disease is caused by the deficiency of
    (a) Mn (b) P
    (c) Mo (d) Zn
125. Deficiency of Mo in citrus plants results in
    (a) Heart rot (b) Khaira disease
    (c) Yellow spots (d) All the above
126. In the diffusion the movement of ions takes place
    (a) From the region of lower concentration to the higher concentration
    (b) From the region of higher concentration to the lower concentration
    (c) Both are correct
    (d) None of the above
127. The metabolic energy is involved in
    (a) Passive uptake (b) Active uptake
    (c) Both are correct (d) None of the above

128. According to the carrier hypothesis the specific carriers are present on
(a) Tonoplast (b) Plasmalemma
(c) Mitochondria (d) Endoplasmic reticulum

129. The cuticular membranes are generally more permeable to
(a) Cations rather than anions (b) Cations and anions both
(c) Anions (d) None of these

130. Scorching or burning on margins of bottom leaves manifests the deficiency of
(a) Zinc (b) Copper
(c) Nitrogen (d) Potassium

131. Which one is an insect trap crop
(a) Bhindi (b) Potato
(c) Paddy (d) Arhar

132. Carbon is an essential element for plant growth plants take it from
(a) Soil (b) Air
(c) Light (d) Water

133. The availability of phosphorus is maximum at soil pH
(a) 5.5-6.5 (b) 7.0
(c) 8.5-6.0 (d) None of these

134. Is potassium takes parts in metabolic activity
(a) May or may not be (b) Yes
(c) No (d) None of the above

135. When a nutrient takes active part in growth and development of plant it is called
(a) Beneficial (b) Essential
(c) Required (d) None of these

136. The first passage through which nutrients enters into the leaves
(a) Intercuticular passage (b) Mesophyll cells
(c) Cell wall plasmic membrane (d) None of above

137. The biological method for determining deficiency of lime, P and k is
(a) Aspergillus niger test (b) Neubavers method
(c) Azotobacter plague test (d) None of the above

138. The neubauer seeding method is used to evaluate the soil fertility. The test plants used in this method is
(a) Rye or oat seedlings (b) Wheat seedlings
(c) Barley seedling (d) All of the above can be used

139. Aspergillus niger test is used fore
(a) Cu and Mg (b) Cu and Zn
(c) Mg and Zn (d) N and S

140. Potassic fertilizer containing maximum quantity of potash is
    (a) Muriate of potash (b) Potassium nitrate
    (c) Potassium ammonium nitrate (d) Sulphate of potash
141. The most efficient use of phosphorus is achieved by
    (a) Broadcasting at the sowing time
    (b) Top dressing 21 days after sowing
    (c) Foliar spray
    (d) Basal placement at the time of sowing
142. Which of the following nutrient is cycled in the soil through atmosphere?
    (a) Potash (b) Nitrogen
    (b) Phosphorus (d) Zinc
143. Coarse grained crops are grown on
    (a) Water logged areas (b) Lowland areas
    (c) High rainfall areas (d) Upland areas
144. Water use efficiency is the highest in case of
    (a) Flood irrigation (b) Drip irrigation
    (c) Sprinkler irrigation (d) Border irrigation
145. Sulphate of potash is preferable to muriate of potash (MOP) for tobacco because
    (a) The chlorine in the MOP increase the nicotine content of tobacco
    (b) The sulphate ion helps to increase the availability of other nutrients
    (c) The chlorine in the MOP affect the burning quality of tobacco
    (d) The application of MOP results in the luxury consumption of potassium
146. Entry of potassium ions into root hair in soils having a low potassium ion content I the soil, is mediated through
    (a) Upper layers of soil
    (b) Mass flow phenomenon
    (c) Utilization of metabolic energy
    (d) Donan equilibrium process
147. Potato tuber is modified form of
    (a) Root (b) Flower
    (c) Leaf (d) Stem
148. Richest source of Nitrogen is
    (a) Dried blood (b) Fish manure
    (c) Dry activated sludge (d) Raw bone meal

149. Browning of cauliflower can be corrected by use of
(a) Boric acid (b) Urea
(c) Zinc sulphate (d) Ammonium molybdate
150. Planting of succeeding crop before harvest of standing crop is known as
(a) Mixed cropping (b) Relay cropping
(c) Multiple cropping (d) Intercropping
151. Soil fertility is reduced due to
(a) Over irrigation (b) Imbalanced use of fertilizer
(c) Poor drainage (d) Continuous cropping
152. The conversion factor of K to $K_2 0$ is
(a) 1.21 (b) 2.21
(c) 1.12 (d) 2.12
153. Organic matter fractionation is formed in
(a) Humus (b) Oil cakes
(c) FYM (d) None of the above
154. Chlorophyll has
(a) Nitrogen (b) Phosphorus
(c) Zinc (d) Calcium
155. Urea is mineralization in the presence of enzyme
(a) Peptidase (b) Urease
(c) Co-enzyme (d) All of the above
156. Calcarious soils are deficit of
(a) Calcium (b) Aluminium
(c) Ferrous (d) None of the above
157. Deficiency of iron results in typical interveinal chiorosis in which
(a) Interveinal area of the older leaves are first affected
(b) Youngest leaves are first affected
(c) Necrotic spots in the inteveinal areas develops
(d) None of the above
158. Whip tail disease is caused by the deficiency of
(a) Mn (b) Mo
(c) Mg (d) S
159. How much farm yard manure s required for obtaining 60 kg of nitrogen for a crop
(a) 140 tonnes (b) 120 tonnes
(c) 160 tonnes (d) 100 tonnes

160. For manufacturing of K_2O which of the following is used
(a) Biotite (b) Kaolinite
(c) Gibssite (d) Pyrite
161. The erosion in which gully width is> 18 meter, depth 3 meter classified as
(a) Small (b) Very small
(c) Medium (d) Deep
162. Acacia catechu can tolerate the pH up to
(a) 9-9.9 (b) 8-8.5
(c) 10-12 (d) 7-8
163. Binding of water with soil is called as
(a) Dispersion (b) Cohesion
(c) Suspension (d) Adhesion
164. Deficiency symptoms of nitrogen occurs first on
(a) Lower leaves (b) Upper leaves
(c) Any where on the plants (d) All of the above
165. Boron deficiency in fodder crops can be seen when boron is
(a) 01.1% (b) 2.3%
(c) <0.1% (d) 1-2%
166. Boron is injurious to plant when irrigational water contains ... concentration of boron
(a) 1-2 ppm (b) 2-3 ppm
(c) >3 ppm (d) 1 ppm
167. Cheap nitrogen per unit volume can be obtained through
(a) Urea (b) Ammonium chloride
(c) CAN (d) Ammonium phosphate
168. How much nitrogen is fixed by Dhaincha crop
(a) 50 kg/ha (b) 70 kg/ha
(c) 30 kg/ha (d) 130 kg/ha
169. Which of following is stem noduling green manuring
(a) Glycoside (b) Synopsis
(c) Sesbilnia rostrata (d) a and b both
170. One ppm means
(a) Part per hundred (b) One part per million
(c) Part per thousand (d) None of these
171. Murate of potash is called
(a) KCl (b) K_2O
(c) $KMnO_4$ (d) $K_2Cr_2O_7$

172. Urea is marketed in the form of
(a) Capsule form (b) Emulsion form
(c) Granular form (d) Dust form
173. Which of the following fertilizer is highly analyzed in nature
(a) DAP (b) Urea
(c) Anhydrous Ammonia (d) None of these
174. The term Agriculture lime means
(a) $CaCO_3$ (b) $Ca(OH)_2$
(c) $CaSO_4$ (d) None of the above
175. Which of the following gas is not found in green houses?
(a) NO_3 (b) CO_2
(c) NO_2 (d) O_2
176. Maximum fixation of K occurs
(a) In 1:2 clay mineral (b) In 2:1 clay mineral
(c) In 1:1 clay mineral (d) In 2.2 clay mineral
177. Alternate wetting and drying in soil, changes
(a) Soil texture (b) Soil temperature
(c) Soil structure (d) Soil colour
178. Which of the following roots are not permanent
(a) Crown roots (b) Seminal roots
(c) Tap roots (d) None of the above
179. In acidic soils toxicity is increased due to increasing
(a) Potassium (b) Aluminium
(c) Sodium (d) Magnesium
180. Plants absorb nutrients because potential of shoots is
(a) Higher than roots (b) Lower than roots
(c) Equal to roots (d) None of the above
181. Which of the following soil have highest water content at wilting coefficient
(a) Sandy loam soils (b) Loam soils
(c) Clay soils (d) Sandy soils
182. In onion smell occur due to presence of
(a) Phosphorus (b) Ferrus
(c) Calcium (d) Sulphur
183. Movement of ions form high concentration to low
(a) Transpiration (b) Diffusion
(c) Evaporation (d) Osmosis

184. Which of the following is non-metallic nutrient
    (a) Magnesium (b) Calcium
    (c) Chloride (d) Boron
185. Chlorosis of the mid rib leaves is caused by
    (a) Zinc (b) Sulphure
    (c) Mn (d) Mg
186. Availability of phosphorus is maximum at
    (a) Neutral (b) Acidic
    (c) Urease (d) Alkaline
187. Weight of top soil of furrow slice will be
    (a) 2.25×10^4 (b) 2.25×10^6
    (c) 2.24×10^{-6} (d) None of the above
188. The term "Contingent Cropping" means
    (a) Crops grown for protecting weather conditions
    (b) Crops grown to achieve nutrition production
    (c) Crops grown to maintain soil fertility
    (d) Crops grown to achieve more soil fertility
189. Green ear disease of bajra is suppressed by increasing the concentration of
    (a) K (b) Ca
    (c) NO_3 (d) P
190. Biological nitrogen fixation is
    (a) Both aerobic and anaerobic process
    (b) Aerobic process
    (c) Anaerobic process
    (d) None of above
191. Efficiency of symbiotic biological nitrogen fixation depends on
    (a) Ecological condition (b) Host characteristics
    (c) Microbial strain characteristics (d) All of the above
192. Denitrification is more in
    (a) Well drained soils (b) Waterlogged soils
    (c) Heavy soils (d) Light soils
193. Til cake contain about –N
    (a) 6.0% (b) 10.2%
    (c) 9.8% (d) 2.5%
194. Cotton seed cakes have about 4% N. 1.9% P, and % K
    (a) 3.5 (b) 1.7
    (c) 4.0 (d) 2.8

195. There is a net increase in the mineralization of organic nitrogen in soil when
(a) C:N ratio is below 20:1
(b) C:N ratio is above 30:1
(c) Nitrogen is taken up by the crops
(d). C:N ratio is 20 to 30.1

196. The elements play direct role in formation of chlorophyll are
(a) Phosphorus and potassium
(b) Nitrogen and magnesium
(c) Calcium and Zinc
(d) Iron and Sulphur

197. The major nutrients are
(a) Fe, Mn, Zn
(b) N, P, K
(c) Cu, Mo, B
(d) Co, Cl, Na

198. Khaira disease of rice is due to the deficiency of
(a) Iron
(b) Zinc
(c) Nitrogen
(d) Calcium

199. Which o the following element is mobile in soil?
(a) N
(b) Mg
(e) K
(d) Ca

200. 95 to 99,5% portion of plant tissues are made up of
(a) N.P and K
(b) Ca, Mg and C
(c) C, H and O
(d) None of these

201. A=B (1-Y) denotes A-value in which A is equal to
(a) Amount of total nutrients in soil
(b) Amount of available nutrients in soil
(c) Amount of unavailable nutrients in soil
(d) None of the above

202. Organic matter influences water holding capacity of soil in the following manner
(a) Is not affected at all
(b) Is stabilized
(c) Is decreased
(d) Is increased

203. Accumulation of carbon dioxide, which is at an especially high level when rice plants are vigorously growing has the following effect on blue green algae
(a) The algae produces phytotoxic metabolites
(b) Nitrogen-fixation by the algae is reduced
(c) N_{2-} fixation by the algae is enhanced
(d) The algae growth is inhabited

204. Urea contain
(a) 24% nitrogen
(b) 60% nitrogen
(c) 16% nitrogen
(d) 46% nitrogen

205. There is a net increase in the mineralization of organic nitrogen in soil when

(a) C:N = 20:1 (b) C:N = 20-30:1
(c) C:N = 30:1 (d) Nitrogen is taken up by the crops

206. The ratio of organic carbon to organic matter in soils is

(a) 1.0:1.7 (b) 20.0:1.0
(c) 1.0:2.0 (a) 1.7:1.0

207. Humus soil contains carbon, oxygen, nitrogen, hydrogen and ash in the ratio of

(a) 10:7:1:1:1 (b) 1:7:10:1:1
(c) 7:10:1:1:1 (a) None of the above

208. Humus soil contains carbon ...

(a) 5 (b) 35
(c) 50 (d) 5

209. Deficiency symptoms of calcium on plants are first noticed at

(a) Low leaves (b) Terminal leaves
(c) Middle leaves (d) All leaves

210. When organic matter is added to the soil

(a) Bulk density does not change
(b) Bulk density is increased
(c) Bulk density is decreased
(d) None of these

211. The availability of molybdenum is more at

(a) pH-5.0 (b) pH-9.0
(c) pH-7.5 (d) pH-7.0

212. The soil is well flocculated if it has more of

(a) Sodium (b) Potassium
(c) Zinc (d) Calcium

213. Complete chlorosis of new Leaves is generally due to the deficiency of nutrient

(a) Zn (b) Mn
(c) Fe (d) Cu

214. In stone fruits the most serious deficiency of micro nutrient is due to

(a) Cu (b) Zn
(c) Mn (d) Fe

215. The soil needed for lawn development should have a pH value of

(a) 5.0-7.5 (b) 5.0-7.0
(c) 5.5-7.0 (d) 5.5-7.5

216. Rock phosphate is used in

(a) Alkaline soil (b) Acidic soil

(c) Neutral soil (d) Saline soil

217. The amount of NPK required to produce 50% of the maximum possible yield is 1 Baule unit which is equal to (in kg/ha)

Nitrogen	P_2O_5	K_2O	Nitrogen	P_2O_5	K_2O
(a) 250	45	60	(b) 223	40	76
(c) 250	40	60	(d) 223	45	76

218. Blossom-end rot in tomato has been found to be caused by the deficiency of

(a) Nitrogen (b) Calcium

(c) Phosphorus (d) Sulphur

219. Affinity of the enzyme RuDP carboxylase for carbon dioxide is enhanced by

(a) Sulphur (b) Phosphorus

(c) Nitrogen (d) Magnesium

220. The sufficiency range of iron is normally between .... .ppm

(a) 50-250 (b) 10-40

(c) 300-400 (d) None of these

221. The presence of ectotrophic mycorrhiza enhances to uptake of nutrients in general, but particularly of

(a) Molybdenum (b) Phosphorus

(c) Calcium (d) Magnesium

222. The quantity of nutrients that can come in direct contact with the plant roots is the amount in a volume of soil .... The volume of roots

(a) Equal to (b) More than

(c) Less than (d) No relation with

223. Which of the following is NOT an essential plant nutrient?

(a) Hydrogen (b) Carbon

(c) Zinc (d) Aluminum

224. ....in 1909 developed an equation that related growth to the supply of plant nutrients

(a) E.A. Mitscherilich (b) RB. McKerchere

(c) V.J. Kilmer (d) J.W. Friedrich

225. The principle similar to that developed by E.A Mitscherilich was also developed several years later by

(a) F. Steenberg (b) J.G. Shannon

(c) M.E. Summer (d) W.J. Spillman

226. The sequence in which amino acids are linked in proteins depends on...
   (a) Climatic control (b) Genetic control
   (c) Agronomical control (d) None of these
227. The tendency of the young, upper leaves to remain as the lower leaves yellow dic is an indication of nitrogen in the plant
   (a) Mobility (b) Stability
   (c) Degradability (d) None of these
228. Build up of soluble sugars and amino acids (due to inadequate potassium); eight compounds encourage the activity of
   (a) Plant hormones (b) Plant pathogens
   (c) Both of these (d) None of these
229. Blossom-end rot in tomato has been found to be caused by the deficiency of
   (a) Nitrogen (b) Calcium
   (c) Phosphorus (d) Suiphure
230. Affinity of the enzyme RuDP carboxylase for carbon dioxide is enhanced by
   (a) Sulphur (b) Phosphorus
   (c) Nitrogen (d) Magnesium
231. The sufficiency range of iron is normally between ... .ppm
   (a) 50-250 (b) 10-40
   (c) 300-400 (d) None of these
232. The presence of ectotrophic mycorrhiza enhances to uptake of nutrients in general, but particularly of
   (a) Molybdenum (b) Phosphorus
   (c) Calcium (d) Magnesium
233. The quantity of nutrients that can come in direct contact with the plant roots is the amount in a volume of soil .... The volume of roots
   (a) Equal to (b) More than
   (c) Less than (d) No relation with
234. ....ion effect represents the effect of adsorbed ion on the release of another from the surface of a colloid
   (a) Complementary (b) Coordinated
   (c) Supplementary (d) Integrated
235. Carbon nitrogen ratio of organic matter is
   (a) 10 to 1 (b) 30 to 2
   (c) 20 to 2 (d) None of the above

236. P_2O_5 is high whereas 1(20 is deficient in which soil
(a) Red soil (b) Alluvial soil
(c) Laterite soil (d) Black cotton soil

237. A soil with 20 me/100g CEC and 5 me/100g exchangeable H will have a base saturation of:
(a) 80% (b) 25%
(c) 75% (d) 133.3%

238. Nitrogen, phosphorus and humus are generally poor in
(a) Laterite soil (b) Alluvial soil
(c) Cotton soil (d) Red soil

239. The maximum phosphorus availability in most of the soils is in the pH range
(a) 4.0-4.5 (b) 7.0-7.5
(c) 6.0-6.5 (d) 5.0-5.5

240. ....generally augments the utilization of phosphorus which is water soluble
(a) Broadcast (b) Broadcast and incorporation
(c) Band placement (d) None of these

241. Rock phosphate is treated with to break the appetite bond and to render the contained phosphate more soluble
(a) Acid alone (b) Alkali alone
(c) Either acid or heat (d) Heat alone

242. Various potassic fertilizers embody nearly an equal effectiveness in situations requiring its supplemental application
(a) Edaphic (b) Cropping
(c) Economic (d) Climatic

243. The concentration of .... ppm of SO_4 ion in the soil or solution cultures have proved adequate for the growth of many plant species
(a) 3-5 (b) 9-11
(c) 1-2 (d) 6-8

244. Proper nourishment for cabbage, potato and sugar beet etc. is essential since these are known to have its high requirement
(a) Zinc (b) Manganese
(c) Sulphure (d) Calcium

245. The essentiality of copper for higher plants was first recognized in
(a) 1921 (b) 1931
(c) 1941 (d) 1911

246. "Reclamation disease" due to copper deficiency occurs in plarts grown on newly reclaimed acid

(a) Histosols (b) Alfisols
(c) Utisols (d) Aridosols

247. Among small grain crops has an exceptional tolerance to low levels of soil copper supply

(a) Barley (b) Rye
(c) Oats (d) Wheat

248. Repeated use of Bordeaux mixture. sewage sludge, pig poultry manures and/or mine wastes may cause toxicity

(a) Iron (b) Aluminum
(c) Copper (d) Zinc

249. A given soil sample contains organic carbon 0.6% phosphorus =0.1%, potassium =1%. The per cent organic matter, P_2O_5 and K_2O contents of the soils is –

Organic matter	P_2O_5	K_2O	Organic matter	P_2O_5	K_2O
(a) 1.02	0.29	1.2	(b) 1.02	0.229	1.2
(c) 1.12	2.29	0.83	(d). 1.7	0.86	0.83

250. The bulk density of a soil with particle density of 2.65 g/cc and pore space 40% would be

(a) 1.29 g/cc (b) 1.59 g/cc
(c) 1.45 g/cc (d) 1.72 g/cc

251. The accessibility and utilization of soil applied copper can be enhanced by

(a) Reducing number of granules
(b) reducing droplets per unit soil volume
(c) Reducing particle size
(d) None of these

252. Each unit increase in pH brings about a decrease in solubility of Fe^{2+} of folds

(a) 75 (b) 150
(c) 50 (d) 100

253. The total soluble iron concentration becomes sufficient to supply iron adequately to roots only at pH ....

(a) 3 (b) 4
(c) 5 (d) 2

254. It has been observed that the iron chelated by sorghum plant metabolites. on a moderately deficient soil, enhanced iron uptake by per cent

(a) 25 (b) 75
(c) 100 (d) 50

255. Nitrogen fertilizer use efficiency in rice can be increased by using
(a) Sulphur coated urea (b) Sulphur coated urea
(c) Blue green algae (d) Urea super granules

256. Which one of the following nutrients plays the most effective role in controlling the rate of transpiration?
(a) Phosphorus (b) Zinc
(c) Potassium (d) Phosphorus

257. Crops during any season are generally able to recover only of the added fertilizer phosphorus
(a) Less than 30% (b) Less than 25%
(c) Less than 35% (d) None of these

258. Potassium salts are
(a) Less mobile than phosphorus (b) Less mobile than nitrates
(c) More mobile than nitrates (d) None of these

259. Broadcast potassium is than banded
(a) More efficient (b) Less efficient than
(c) As efficient as (d) None of these

260. Winter application of phosphorus is followed by
(a) Warm areas (b) Both of these
(c) Cool areas (d) None of these

261. Potassium is utilized more efficiently if applied
(a) Before/at planning (b) Side dressed
(c) Top dressed (d) None of these

262. Amongst micronutrients application of which one of the following has become necessary in paddy crop in north India
(a) Iron (b) Zinc
(c) Boron (d) Copper

263. Availability o phosphorus to crop plants is most effected by
(a) Soil pH (b) Temperature
(c) Biological factors (d) Soil moisture 'stress

264. Nitrogen in DAP is
(a) 36% (b) 9%
(c) 18% (d) 46%

265. In mustard crop gypsum is applied to supply
(a) Sulphur (b) Calcium
(c) Nitrogen (d) Zinc

266. Among oilcakes the highest nitrogen content is in
(a) Neem cake (b) Castor cake
(c) Coconut cake (d) Groundnut cake

267. Symptoms of iron deficiency in plants are
    (a) Yellowing of whole plant
    (b) Drying of lower leaves
    (c) Yellowing of lower leaves
    (d) Yellowing of young growing leaves
268. Opening of stomata is related with
    (a) Potassium (b) Iron
    (c) Calcium (d) Magnesium
269. Non-essential but useful nutrients for plants would include
    (a) Vanadium and Sodium (b) Vanadium and Chlorine
    (c) Carbon and Vanadium (d) Sodium and Chlorine
270. Which one of the following nitrogen factors would bring down wide C:N ratio material of 100: L to the desirable C:N ratio of 40:1 for compost making ?
    (a) 1.5 (b) 2.5
    (c) 2.0 (d) 1.0
271. Which of the following elements is part of the chlorophyll ?
    (a) Iron (b) Magnesium
    (c) Zinc (d) Manganese
272. Which of the following mineral elements is essential for nitrogen metabolism in green plants?
    (a) P (b) Zn
    (c) Mo (d) K
273. Which element is immobile in the plants?
    (a) Potassium (b) Nitrogen
    (c) Calcium (d) Phosphorus
274. What is the upper crops tolerable limit of biurett in urea ?
    (a) 1.5% (b) 0.5%
    (c) 1.0% (d) 3.0%
275. The addition of excess soluble phosphatic fertilizers to soil may affect plant growth by
    (a) Inhibiting the growth of microorganisms
    (b) Reducing the availability of zinc
    (c) Reducing the availability, the concentration of plant nutrients
    (d) Precipitating iron and aluminium
276. Which one of the following concentrated organic manures has maximum phosphorus'?
    (a) Fish meal (b) Guano
    (c) Steral meal (d) Poultry manual

277. The nitrogenous fertilizer manufactured in India which occupies the first place in production today is
(a) Urea (b) Ammonium phosphate
(c) Ammonium sulpahte (d) Calcium ammonium nitrate
278. Which one of the following fertilizers is least hygroscopic
(a) Ammonium sulpabte (b) Calcium ammonium nitrate
(c) Ammonium phosphate (d) Urea
279. Which one of the following fertilizers is least hygroscopic
(a) Ammonium sulpahte (b) Diammonium phosphate
(c) Calcium ammonium nitrate (d) Urea
280. Diamnionium phosphate requirement for supplying 45 kg N and 115 kg P_2O_4 to one hectare peanut crop is
(a) 150 kg (b) 250 kg
(c) 200 kg (d) 100 kg
281. Fruit formation is suppressed due to deficiency of
(a) Boron (b) Magnesium
(c) Sulphur (d) Calcium
282. Carryover fertilizer effects are more pronounced in the case of
(a) Urea (b) Calcium ammonium nitrate
(c) Ammonium nitrate (d) Single super phosphate
283. Water drains by gravitational force from pores larger than
(a) About 30-60 microns (b) About 10-20 microns
(c) About 20-30 microns (d) None of the above
284. Soils with high pH are generally deficient in
(a) Zn & Mn (b) Ca & Mg
(c) B & Fe (d) Cu & Mo
285. Which one of the following plant nutrients is useful in increasing resistance to diseases and insect-pests
(a) Calcium (b) Potassium
(c) Phosphorus (d) Nitrogen
286. Use of materials like sulphur. polform UF. isobutylidene diurea etc. improves fertilizer use efficiency. When such additives are used, the N-fertilizers are termed as
(a) Prilled urea
(b) Controlled release nitrogenous fertilizer
(c) Slow nitrifring N-fertilizer
(d) Complex fertilizer

287. Essential elements are those
    (a) Which could be replaced by other elements with similar properties
    (b) Which are required in large quantities
    (c) Whose deficiency would prevent the completion of plant's life cycle
    (d) Which would promote plant growth
288. Molybdenum is required by plants because it is a cofactor
    (a) Cytohrome oxidase (b) Phosphatase
    (c) Nitrite reductase (d) Nitrate reductase
289. The average chemical composition of NPK percentage of night soil is
    (a) 0.5-0.6-0.5 (b) 3.7-4.0-2.0
    (c) 2.0-2.6-0.5 (d) 5.5-4.0-2.0
290. The residual effect of ammonical nitrogenous fertilizer in soil as
    (a) Alkaline (b) Acidic
    (c) Neutral (d) None of these
291. Urea is mineralized in the presence of enzyme
    (a) Peptase (b) Urease
    (c) Co-enzyme (d) All the above
292. When you apply 80 kg N/ha to wheat crop how many kg of urea would be required
    (a) 120.00 kg (b) 80.00 kg
    (c) 173.91 kg (d) 100.25 kg
293. Single super phosphate (SSP) is manufactured from
    (a) Rock phosphate (b) Bone meal
    (c) Di-calcium phosphate (d) None of the above
294. Geological weathering takes place in
    (a) Upper layers of soil (b) Lower layers of soil
    (c) On earth crust (d) None of the above
295. Bone meal is well suited for
    (a) Alkaline soil (b) Neutral soil
    (c) Acidic Soil (d) All of these
296. Til cake contain about –N
    (a) 6.0% (b) 10.2%
    (c) 9.8% (d) 2.5%
297. Cotton seed cakes have about 4% N, 1.9% P, and .... % K
    (a) 3.5 (b) 1.7
    (c) 4.0 (d) 2.8

298. The elements play direct role in formation of chlorophyll are
(a) Phosphorus and potassium (b) Nitrogen and magnesium
(c) Calcium and Zinc (d) Iron and Sulphur

299. The major nutrients are
(a) Fe, Mn, Zn (b) N, P, K
(c) Cu, Mo. B (d) Co, Cl, Na

300. Khaira disease of rice is due to the deficiency of
(a) Iron (b) Zinc
(c) Nitrogen (d) Calcium

301. Deficiency symptoms of calcium on plants are first noticed at
(a) Low leaves (b) Terminal leaves
(c) Middle leaves (d) All leaves

302. When organic matter is added to the soil
(a) Bulk density does not change (b) Bulk densit is increased
(c) Bulk density is decreased (d) None of these

303. The availability of molybdenum is more at
(a) pH-5.0 (b) pH-6.0
(c) pH-7.5 (d) pH-7.0

304. The soil is well flocculated if it has more of
(a) Sodium (b) Potassium
(c) Zinc (d) Calcium

305. Complete chlorosis of new leaves is generally due to the deficiency of nutrient
(a) Zn (b) Mn
(c) Fe (d) Cu

306. In stone fruits the most serious deficiency of micro nutrient is due to
(a) Cu (b) Zn
(c) Mn (d) Fe

307. The soil needed for lawn development should have a pH value of
(a) 5.0-7.5 (b) 5.0-7.0
(c) 5.5-7.0 (d) 5.5-7.5

308. Rock phosphate is used in
(a) Alkaline soil (b) Acidic soil
(c) Neutral soil (d) Saline soil

309. In saline-alkali soil the electrical conductivity is
(a) 2 dS/m (b) >4 dS/m
(c) 3 dS/m (d) None of these

310. Soils with high pH are generally deficient in
   (a) Zn and Mn (b) Ca and Mg
   (c) B and Fe (d) Cu and Mo
311. Which one of the following minerals is least weatherable in soil?
   (a) Olline (b) Quartz
   (c) Biotite (d) Calcite
312. The amount of NPK required to produce 50% of the maximum possible yield is 1 Baule unit which is equal to (in kg/ha)

Nitrogen	P_2O_5	K_2O	Nitrogen	P_2O_5	K_2O
(a) 250	45	60	(b) 223	40	76
(c) 250	40	60	(d) 223	45	76

313. Carbon nitrogen ratio of organic matter is
   (a) 10 to 1 (b) 30 to 2
   (c) 20 to 2 (d) None of the above
314. P_2O_5 is high whereas K_2O is deficient in which soil
   (a) Red soil (b) Alluvial soil
   (c) Latente soil (d) Black cotton soil
315 A soil with 20 me/100g CEC and 5 me/100 g exchangeable H will have a base saturation of
   (a) 80% (b) 25%
   (c) 75% (d) 133.3%
316. Nitrogen, phosphorus and humus are generally poor in
   (a) Laterite soil (b) Alluvial soil
   (c) Cotton soil (d) Red soil
317. The soil which is comparable with the chernozems of Russia and the praine soils of the cotton growing slates of the cotton growing states of the USA especially the black adobe of California
   (a) Alluvial soil (b) Red soil
   (c) Black soil (d) Laterite soil
318. Which one of the following microorganisms is involved in nitrification in the soil
   (a) Micrococcus (b) Thiobacillus
   (c) Pseudomonas (d) Nitrosomonas
319. The unit of fertilizer or any other growth factor which is necessary to produce the yield which in 50% of maximum possible yield is called
   (a) Fertilizer unit (b) Standard unit
   (c) Optimum unit (d) Baule unit

320. Which of the following fertilizer has maximum plant nutrient
   (a) Murate of potash (b) DAP
   (c) TSP (d) Ammonium nitrate
321. Process of immobilization refers to
   (a) Conversion of inorganic from to organic form
   (b) Conversion of N-compounds to protein
   (c) Conversion of organic from to inorganic from
   (d) None of above
322. Ammonium Sulphate contains........N
   (a) 49% (b) 20%
   (c) 42% (d) 46%
323. What is the P_2O_5 content of various rock phosphates
   (a) 20-35% (b) 49%
   (c) 11-20% (d) 18-20%
324. Which nutrient is maximum given for raising the field
   (a) Nitrogen (b) Phosphorus
   (c) Potash (d) Calcium
325. The fertilizers which have two or more than two major plant nutrient in their chemical composition are called
   (a) Complex fertilizer (b) Organic fertilizer
   (c) Double fertilizer (d) Mixed fertilizer
326. The organic matter content of Indian peat and marshy soil is
   (a) >10% (b) 10-40%
   (c) >40% (d) None of above
327. The availability of phosphorus is optimum in the pH range of
   (a) <7 (b) 6-8
   (c) 5-8 (d) 7-8
328. Which of the following would one find in a submerged rice field?
   (1) Reduced state (2) Ammonical nitrogen (3) Ferrous sulphide
   (a) 3 alone (b) 1 & 3
   (c) 1 alone (d) 1, 2 & 3
329. Water use efficiency is defined as
   (a) Economic yield per unit of irrigation water applied
   (b) Ratio of water used by the crop to the irrigation water applied
   (c) Ratio of net irrigation to gross irrigation including other losses
   (d) Dry matter produced per unit of water used by the crop

330. Gross water requirement of a crop is the
   (a) Total available water, which is present in the soil profile during the crop period
   (b) Same as total rainfall in the crop period under heavy rainfall areas
   (c) Evaporation and water used by the crop its metabolic activities
   (d) Sum of net irrigation requirement, effective rainfall and other unavoidable losses during irrigation

331. Organic matter content under well-drained conditions is higher under
   (a) Field crops (b) Grasslands
   (c) Forest covers (d) Fruit crops

332. The.............oxidation of ammonium has been termed as nitrification
   (a) Biological (b) Chemical
   (c) Physical (d) Physio-chemical

333. ....is considered to be most important of the soil organics bringing about the conversion of NH_4 to NO_2
   (a) Azotobacter (b) Azospilrillum
   (c) Nitrobacter (d) Nitrosomonas

334. The rapid increase in dentrification at the elevated soil temperatures suggests that ......microorganisms play a major role in denitrification
   (a) Cherhophilic (b) Photophilic
   (c) Hydrophilic (d) Thermophilic

335. .... Of the NH_4 in a region of alkaline micro site helps to restore the conditions suitable for the normal conversion of NO_2 to NO_3
   (a) Dilution (b) Diffusion
   (c) Both of these (d) None of these

336. The losses of ammonia usually become greater with
   (a) Decrease in calcium (b) Decrease in temperature
   (c) Decrease in soil pH (d) Increase in soil pH

337. The highest percentage content of nitrogen among the commonly used nitrogenous fertilizers es embodied by
   (a) Ammonium Nitrate (b) Urea Sulphate
   (c) Urea (d) Anhydrous ammonia

338. Permissible biuret level in most of urea fertilizers is .... percent
   (a) 4 (b) 2
   (c) 3 (d) 5

339. In the fertilized soil with soil solution concentration of one ppm of phosphorus, mass flow contribution to phosphorus nutrition of crops could approach .... percent
   (a) 40 (b) 0
   (c) 30 (d) 20

340. The quantity of solid phase phosphorus that acts as reserve is often referred to as ....
(a) Intensity factor (b) Quality factor
(c) Quantity factor (d) None of these

341. Phosphate enzymes play a major role in ..... of organic phosphate in soil
(a) Immobilization (b) Mass transportation
(c) Mineralization (d) None of these

342. The mineralization of organic phosphorus has been studied in relation to .... ratio
(a) C/N/S (b) C/N/P
(c) C/N/K (d) C/N/Ca

343. Clays such as Kaolinite will fix larger quantities of phosphorus with .... SiO_2/R_2O_3 ratio
(a) High (b) Low
(c) Equal (d) None of these

344. Amorphous aluminosilicate minerals like allophone have .... negative charge which is partly of entirely balanced by complex aluminum cations
(a) Zero (b) Large
(c) Small (d) None of these

345. A minor portion of the phosphorus sorption capacity of soils originates from
(a) Sodium bicarbonate (b) Calcium carbonate
(c) Calcium oxide (d) Sodium bicarbonate

346. The maximum phosphorus availability in most of the soils is in the pH range.........
(a) 4.0-4.5 (b) 7.0-7.5
(c) 6.0-6.5 (d) 5.0-5.5

347. ....generally augments the utilization og phosphorus which is water soluble
(a) Broadcast (b) Broadcast and incorporation
(c) Band placement (d) None of these

348. Rock phosphate is treated with ...... to break the appetite bond and to render the contained phosphate more soluble
(a) Acid alone (b) Alkalli alone
(c) Either acid or heat (d) Heat alone

349. Various potassic fertilizers embody nearly an equal effectiveness in .... situtations requiring its supplement application
(a) Edaphic (b) Cropping
(c) Economic (d) Climatic

350. The concentration of ……. ppm of SO_4 ion in the soil or solution cultures have proved adequate for the growth of many plant supecies
   (a) 3-5 (b) 9-11
   (c) 1-2 (d) 6-8
351. Proper ……. Nourishment for cabbage, potato and sugar beet etc. is essential since these are known to have its high requirement
   (a) Zinc (b) Manganese
   (c) Sulphure (d) Calcium
352. The essentiality of copper for higher plants was first recognized in….
   (a) 1921 (b) 1931
   (c) 1941 (d) 1911
353. "Reclamation disease" due to copper deficiency occurs in plants grown on newly reclaimed acid ……..
   (a) Histosols (b) Alfisols
   (c) Utisols (d) Aridosols
354. Among small grain crops …… has an exceptional tolerance to low levels of soil copper supply
   (a) Barely (b) Rye
   (c) Oats (d) Wheat
355. Reapeated use of Brodeaux mixture, sewage sludge, pig poultry manures and/or mine wastes may cause …….. toxicity
   (a) Iron (b) Aluminium
   (c) Copper (d) Zinc
356. A given soil sample contains organic carbon=0.6% phosphorus=0.1% potassium=1%. The percent organic matter, P_2O_5 and K_2O contents of the soils is

Organic matter	P2O5	K2O	Organic matter	P2O5	K2O
(a) 1.02	0.29	1.2	(b) 1.02	0.221	1.2
(c) 1.12	2.29	.83	(d) 1.7	.86	.83

357. The bulk density of a soil with particle density of 2.65 g/cc and pore spade 40% would be
   (a) 1.29 g/cc (b) 1.59 g/cc
   (c) 1.45 g/cc (d) 1.72 g/cc
358. The accessibility and utilization of soil applied copper can be enhanced by ………
   (a) Reducing number of granules
   (b) Reducing droplets per unit soil volume
   (c) Reducing particle size
   (d) None of these

359. Each unit increas in pH brings about a decrease in solubility of Fe^{2+} of …… folds
(a) 75 (b) 150
(c) 50 (d) 100

360. The total solube iron concentration becomes sufficient to supply iron adequately to roots only at pH…….
(a) 3 (b) 4
(c) 5 (d) 2

361. It has been observed that the iron chelated by sorghum plant meatabolites, on a moderately deficient soil, enhanced iron uptake by ………percent
(a) 25 (b) 75
(c) 100 (d) 50

362. There can actually be a build up of toxic concentration of Fe^{2+} in the soil solution of
(a) Aridsol (b) Latosol
(c) Histosol (d) Vertisol

363. For each unit increase in pH, the concentration of Mn^{2+} decreased by ……… folds
(a) 100 (b) 150
(c) 50 (d) 200

364. Silicon is the ….. most abundant element in the earth crust
(a) Third (b) Sixth
(c) Second (d) Fourth

365. Properties of the silicon deficient Hqaiah Soils include
(a) High base saturation (b) High total silicon
(c) High pH (d) High total aluminium content

366. It is generally accepted that the Gramineae members contain ……… times the silicon concentratioin normally found in legumes and other dicotyledonous plants
(a) 10-20 (b) 20-30
(c) 05-10 (d) 30-40

367. Nitrogen fertilizer use efficiency in rice can be increased by using
(a) Sulphur coated urea (b) Sulphur coated urea
(c) Blue green alage (d) Urea super granules

368. Which one of the f ollowing nutriens plays the most effective role in controlling the rate transpiration?
(a) Phosphorus (b) Zinc
(c) Potassium (d) Phophorus

369. Crops during any season are generally able to recover only ..... of the added fertilizer phophorus
    (a) Less than 30% (b) Less than 25%
    (c) More mobile than nitrates (d) None of these
370. Potassium salts are
    (a) Less mobile than phosphorus (b) Less mobile tha nitrates
    (c) More mobile tha nitrate (d) None of these
371. Broadcast potassium is ...... than banded
    (a) More efficient (b) Less effficient than
    (c) As efficient as (d) None of these
372. Winter application of phosphorus is followed by ....
    (a) Warm areas (b) Both of these
    (c) Cool areas (d) None of these
373. Potassium is utilized more efficiently if applied ....
    (a) Before/at planning (b) Side dressed
    (c) Top dressed (d) None of these
374. Tillage of the soil .... rate of disappearance of organic matter
    (a) Increases (b) Maintains
    (c) Reduces (d) Has no effect
375. Amongst micronutrients application of which one of the following has become necessary in paddy crop in North India
    (a) Iron (b) Zinc
    (c) Boron (d) Copper
376. Availability O Phosphorus to crop plants is most effected by
    (a) Soil pH (b) Temperature
    (c) Biological factors (d) Soil moisture stress
377. Nitrogen in DAP is
    (a) 36% (b) 9%
    (c) 18% (d) 46%
378. In mustard crop gypsum is applied to supply
    (a) Sulphur (b) Calcium
    (c) Nitrogen (d) Zinc
379. Among oilcake the highest nitrogen content is in
    (a) Neem cake (b) Castor cake
    (c) Coconut cake (d) Groundnut cake
380. In saline soil major problemis due to
    (a) High exchangeable sodium (b) Low soil pH
    (c) High pH (d) High content of soluble salts

381. Symptpoms of iron deficiency in plants are
(a) Yellowing of whole plant
(b) Drying of lower leaves
(c) Yellowing of lower leaves
(d) Yellowing of young growing leaves

382. Opening of stomata is related with
(a) Potassium (b) Iron
(c) Calcium (d) Magnesium

383. Which of the following adsorbed cations arelargely responsible for soil acidity
(a) Hydrogen (b) Sodium
(c) Calcium (d) Aluminium

384. Which of the following soils have electrical conductivity less than 4 ds/m
(a) Acid (b) Saline
(c) Saline-sodic (d) Sodic

385. Which of the following are sensitive crops
(a) Barley (b) Onion
(c) Potato (d) Sugarbeet

386. Which of the following are meta morphic rocks
(a) Schist (b) Slate
(c) Dolomite (d) Shales

387. Per cent pore space can not be calculated correctly by

(a) Bulk density% pore space =% pore space = $\frac{\text{Bulk density}}{\text{Particle density}} \times 100$

(b) % pore space = 100% solid

(c) Bulk density% pore space =% pore space = $\frac{\text{Bulk density}}{\text{Particle density}} \times 100$

(d) Bulk density% pore space =% pore space = $\frac{\text{Bulk density}}{2.65\ g/cm^2} \times 100$

388. The earth worm csats care definitely higher in ....than the soil
(a) Bacteria (b) Organic matter
(c) Available nutrients (d) All of these

389. Development of acid soils in humid areas is largely associated with
(a) Intense weathering (b) Leaching out of basic cations
(c) Oxidation of pyrite (d) Use of poor quality irrigation water

390. Which one of the following nitrogen factors would bring down wide C:N ratio material of 100:a to the desirable C:N ratio 40:1 for compost making?
(a) 1.5 (b) 2.5
(c) 2.0 (d) 1.0

391. Which of the following elements is part of the chlorophy II?
(a) Iron (b) Megnesium
(c) Zinc (d) Maganese

392. Which of the following mineral elements is essential for nitrogen metabolism in green plants?
(a) P (b) Zn
(c) Mo (d) K

393. Which element is immobile in the plants?
(a) Potassium (b) Nitrogen
(c) Calcium (d) Phosphorus

394. What is the upper crops tolerable limit of non biurett in urea?
(a) 1.5% (b) 0.5%
(c) 1.0% (d) 3.0%

395. The crop plants transpire more when there is
(a) High temperature and low humidity
(b) High humidity and high wind velocity
(c) High temperature and high humidity
(d) Low temperature and low humidity

396. An organism which converts nitrite to Nitrate is
(a) Azotobactor (b) Nitrobactor
(c) Nitrosomonas (d) Phosphorus

397. The efficiency of field irrigation would be more in
(a) Sandy loam (b) Loam
(c) Clay loam (d) Heavy loam

398. Which one of the following occupies the highest volume percent in a fine sandy loam surface soil in good condition, for plant growth?
(a) Organic matter
(b) Mineral matter
(c) Pore space which includes air and/or water
(d) Other including macro and micro flora and fauna

399. Pedology considers soil as a
   (a) Natural body
   (b) Medium for plant growth
   (c) Powdered rock mass of the earth's crust
   (d) Purely a synthesized one
400. The fundamental role of root hairs in plants is
   (a) To absorb water and mineral salts from the soil
   (b) To bind soil particles to the root for firm fixation o the plant
   (c) To product the young root from damage by coarse soil particles
   (d) To protect he root from soil microbes
401. Water and mineral salts are translocated in plants in the
   (a) Xylem (b) Phloem
   (c) Collenchyma (d) Porechymal 1, 2 & 4
402. The layers in soil are referred to as
   (a) Hard pans (b) Horizons
   (c) Profile (d) Pedocals
403. Chlorites are basically silicates of
   (a) Aluminium with some magnesium and aluminium
   (b) Iron and Aluminium
   (c) Magnesium with some iron and aluminium
   (d) Iron with some magnesium and aluminium
404. The cation excahnge capacity of a mineral soil containing predominately kaloniticclay minerals generally ranges between
   (a) 80-100me e per 10 gm, soil
   (b) More hen 100 m.e. per 100gm soil
   (c) 3.15 m.e. per 100g soil
   (d) 15-40 m.e. per 100gm soil
405. In soil science micelle stands for
   (a) Negatively charged silt particles with high CEC
   (b) Collodial panicle carrying positive charge
   (c) Micropores in between textural particles
   (d) Colloidal particle carrying negative change
406. Soils high in swelling clays which crack widely upon drying resulting in shrinking, shearing and soil mass movement are characteristics of
   (a) Podzols (b) Entisols
   (c) Ultisols (d) Vertisols

407. Which one of the following micro-organisms is responsible for maximum nutrient cycling in the soil?
(a) Fungi (b) Actinomycetes
(c) Bacteria (d) Algae

408. Which state is devoid of arid zone?
(a) Madhya Pradesh (b) Andhra Pradesh
(c) Punjab (d) Maharashtra

409. If the nitrogen content in crop residues is less than 2% than
(a) Net immobilization will take place
(b) Partial mineralization will take place
(c) Net mineralization will take place
(d) None of the above

410. 'Whiptail' symptom in cauliflower is due to the deficiency of
(a) Iron (b) Molybenum
(c) Zinc (d) Copper

411. The number of essential elements required for the growth of most higher plants is
(a) 8 (b) 16
(c) 8 (d) 3

412. Which one of the following is not a component of the moisture potential in soils
(a) Turgor potential (b) Osmotic potential
(c) Gravity potential (d) Metric potential

413. Crop logging is the method of
(a) Soil fertalitu evaluation
(b) Assessing crop damage
(c) Testing suitability of fertilizer
(d) Plant analysis of assessing requirement of nutrients for crop production

414. In a composed pit, the hea of combustion of organic matter raises the temperature when decay is occuring rapidly during decay, the temperature rise by
(a) 75-90° C (b) 40-60° C
(c) 60-80° C (d) 50-72° C

415. The maximum irrigation efficiency percent age is found in which class of soil?
(a) Sandy soil (b) Loamy soil
(c) Clay loam (d) Heavy clay

416. The biofertilizer like blue-green algae recommended for cultivation of 1ha paddy crop is
(a) 5-10 (b) 10-15
(c) 25-30 (d) 15-20

417. The total and area on a water way that contributes run off water to the flow at the point is known as
(a) Water Conservvation (b) Watershed
(c) Soil conservation (d) All of these

418. Mixed cropping provides
(a) Almost a complete protection against soil erosion
(b) Better and continuous cover land
(c) Good protection against the beating action of the rain
(d) Assurance of one or more crops to the form

419. Which of the following grasses can be used for prevention soil erosion by
(a) Cynodon dactylon (b) Dianthuim annulatum
(c) Cenchrus ciliaris (d) All of these

420. Which of the following examples of erosion permitting corp?
(a) Pearlmillet (b) Sorghum
(c) Maize (d) All of these

421. Contour bunding is useful as it
(a) Increase utter level's in the wells
(b) Increases yield of crops in dry farming areas in Maharashtra
(c) Increase employment opportunities
(d) All of the above

422. Rhizobium culture is generally used for
(a) Cash crops (b) Cereals
(c) Legume crop (d) All of these

423. The first entry and movement of water through the soil surface is known as
(a) Gravitational law (b) Percolation
(c) Infilatration (d) None of these

424. The most important strip cropping practices in controlling erosion and conserving water is
(a) Field strip cropping (b) Contour strip croping
(c) Wind strip (d) All of these

425. Poor nitrificationrate of non-edible mahua (Madhucal Lattifolia) cake is due to
(a) Wide C:N ratio (b) The presence of oil
(c) Low nitrogen content (d) The presence of certain alkaloids

426. Which of the following pairs is correctly matched

Fertilizers Nutrient Content

(a) Urea 42.0 (%N)

(b) Diammonium phosphate 20.2 (% P)

(c) Muriate of Potash 47.5 (%K)

(d) Ammonium sulphate 21.5 (%N)

427. The neutralizing values of the following limiting materials are such that

(a) $CaCo_3$>CaO>$Ca(OH)_2CaMg(CO_3)_2$

(b) CaO>Ca(OH)2>CaCO3>$CaMg(CO3)_2$

(c) $Ca(OH)_2$>CaO>$CaMg(Co_3)_2$>$CaCO_3$

(d) CaO>$Ca(OH)_2$>$CaMg(Co_3)_2$>$CaCO_3$

428. The nitrogenous fertilizer of choice for tea is

(a) Urea (b) Calcium ammonium nitrate

(c) Ammonium sulphate (d) Ammonium nitrate

429. Transport of phosphate from the cytosol (pH about 7.0) into vacuoles (pHnearly 5.5) involves

(a) (H_2PO_4) alone (b) (HPO_4) and $(HPO_4)^2$

(c) $(HPO_4)^2$ alone (d) $(PO_4)^3$ lone

430. If the slope of the land is increased 4 times the velocity of water flowing over it is approximately double and capacity of water is increased about

(a) 2-time (b) 8-time

(c) 4-time (d) 6-time

431. The nitrogen fixing bacteria are

(a) Azospirillum (b) Rhizobium

(c) Azotobacter (d) All of the above

432. Magnesium is necessary for

(a) Chlorophy II (b) Plasma

(c) Plastids (d) None of these

433. Biofertilizer is a

(a) Mixture of inorganic fertilizer and microorganism

(b) Decomposed compost enriched with mineral solubilising bacteria

(c) Mixture of inorganic matter and microorganism

(d) Culture having the desired strain of microorganism

434. The mechanism of the crop plants in operation in the soil water plant system is/as follows

(a) Diffusion

(b) The constant exchange and root inter ception

(c) The mass flow or convection

(d) All of the above

435. Diminished carbohydrate status of the placed under high nitrogen supply is due to
(a) Lower Photosynthetic activity (b) Increased transpiration ratio
(c) Increassed vegetative growth (d) Vigorous protien synthesis
436. Consider the following symtoms
(1) Effect more pronounced on shoots when compared to roots and cruciferious plants develop narrow leaf lamina
(2) Blockage of the synthasis of cystine, methionine etc.
(3) Younger leaves shows signs of deficiency first
(4) High amide and nitrate nitrogen
Development of the above mentioned symptoms is attributable to the deficiency of
(a) Calcium (b) Magnesium
(c) Sulphur (d) Nitrogen
437. Gully-erison affects 2.3 million ha in India which occurs because of
(a) Carrying out mechanical measures
(b) Bad management of land resources
(c) Designing of various structures
(d) All of the above
438. The vegetative development of plants by imparting a healthy green colour to leave is done by
(a) Nitrogen (b) Potassium
(c) Phosphorus (d) None of these
439. The influence on vigour of plants and formation of metacells etc. is done by the
(a) Phosphorus (b) Potassium
(c) Nitrogen (d) None of these
440. In saline soil exchangeable sodium percentage is less than
(a) 11 (b) 17
(c) 15 (d) 23
441. The length of spillway is determined by the formula of
(a) Q=1.70 LH 3×2 (b) Q=17.0 LH_3×2
(c) =1.70LH3 (d) None of these
Here Q=ru-off in cubic meters/sec; L= Length in m of water flow above the spillway level
442. The tolerant spp. Able grow over 5000 ppm salts is
(a) Barley (b) Sugarcane
(c) Datepalm (d) All of the above

443. In non-saline alkaline or sodic soils the Electrical conductivity (EC) is less than

(a) 2 dSm^{-1} (b) 8 dAm^{-1}

(c) 6 dSm^{-1} (d) 4 dSm^{-1}

444. Any system of gullies an independent catchment with a regular stream which is called

(a) Nomenclature (b) Irrigation

(c) Drainage system (d) None of these

445. For preparing a mixed fertilizer, 100 kg of ammonium sulphate and 125 kg of single super phosphate were mixed and 25 kg of filler was added to this mixture in terms of N-P_2O_5-K_2O_2 the fertilizer of choice would be

(a) 10-10-0 (b) 5-10-0

(c) 8-8-0 (d) 5-5-0

446. Father of Soil testing

(a) M.L.Troug (b) Liebig

(c) Black (d) Marshall

447. For each degree °C rise in temperature than increase EC

(a) 1% (b) 2%

(c) 3% (d) 4%

448. Total salt content in solution in ppm

(a) EC (dS/m) at 25° C (b) EC (dS/m) at 25° C × 0.36

(c) EC (dS/m) at 25° C × 640 (d) EC (dS/m) at 25° C × 10

449. To determination of EC use the reagent

(a) 0.01 N KCl (b) 0.1 N KCl

(c) 0.01 N H_2SO_4 (d) None of these

450. To determination of pH use the Buffer solution

(a) pH 4.0 (b) pH 7.0

(c) pH 9.0 (d) All of these

451. Determination of calcium and magnesium use the indicator

(a) Methyl orange (b) Eriochrome black T (EBT)

(c) Phenolphthalein indicator (d) Mixed indicator

452. Determination of carbonates and bicarbonates use the indicator

(a) Methyl orange (b) Phenolphthalein indicator

(c) Both a and b (d) Mixed indicator

453. Sodium is estimated by flame photometer in a

(a) Blue flame (b) Red flame

(c) White flame (d) Violet flame

454. Ca and Mg in the solution is determined by
(a) Flame photometer (b) AAS
(c) Both a and b (d) None

455. For accurate pH measurement, which of the used
(a) Colour Chart (b) pH meter
(c) pH strips (d) Dye solution

456. Determination of chloride use the indicator
(a) Methyl orange (b) Phenolphthalein indicator
(c) Methyl red (d) Potassium chromate

457. If pH decrease by one unit, than decrease in voltage
(a) 0.59 mV (b) 0.059 mV
(c) 59.1 mV (d) 5.9 mV

458. Determination of organic carbon use the indicator
(a) Methyl orange (b) Phenolphthalein indicator
(c) Mixed indicator (d) Diphenylamine indicator

459. Organic carbon content of soil is estimated by the method
(a) Colorimetric method (b) Titrimetric method
(c) Both a and b (d) None of these

460. Mohr's salt is known as
(a) 0.5 N Ferrous Ammonium Sulphate
(b) 1N Potassium dichromate
(c) Mixed indicator
(d) Diphenylamine indicator

461. Organic carbon content of soil is estimated by the method
(a) Colorimetric method (b) Titrimetric method
(c) Both a and b (d) None of these

462. When diacid mixture is used for digestion of plant sample, those elements cannot be determined from that extract is
(a) S (b) K
(c) P (d) N

463. The dye used for titrimetric determination of ascorbic acid is
(a) Para Nitro phenol
(b) 2,4- dinitrophenol
(c) 2-6 di chloro phenol iudophenol
(d) 2,6 dibromo phenol indophenol

464. At which wavelength plant phosphorus can be estimated on Uy-vis spectrophotometer?
(a) 440 nm (b) 660 nm
(e) 470 nm (d) 570 nm

465. Determination of Fe, Mn, Zn, and Cu from plant is done by using
(a) FPM (b) SPM
(c) AAS (d) EC meter

466. 'ppb=
(a) mg/ml (b) g/ml
(c) mg/1 (d) g/1

467. The salt used along with $CuSO_4$ and $FeSO_4$ as digestion mixture used for N estimation is
(a) $MgSO_4$ (b) K_2SO_4
(c) Na_25O_4 (d) $ZnSO_4$

468. Optical Density =
(a) 2-logT (b) Log -2T
(c) 2log–T (d) T-log2

469. Soil testing has proved to be most beneficial for
(a) Annual crops (b) Orchards
(c) Voneyards (d) Pastures

470. Which sampling schedule would result in the most accurate soil tests for a new crop?
(a) Sampling immediately after harvest
(b) Sampling as soon as the soil freezes in the fall
(c) Sampling as soon as the soil thaws in the spring
(d) Sampling as close as possible to the time of planting

471. Soil testing
(a) Is a method to know about cropping season
(b) A procedure of multiple cropping
(c) Determines the fertility status of soil
(d) All of the above

ANSWERS

1(a) 2(c) 3(a) 4(a) 5(c) 6(b) 7(a) 8(c) 9(b) 10(c) 11(a) 12(b) 13(b) 14(b) 15(c) 16(a) 17(c) 18(b) 19(b) 20(d) 21(c) 22(c) 23(a) 24(b) 25(b) 26(d) 27(d) 28(c) 29(b) 30(a) 31(b) 32(a) 33(b) 34(d) 35(a) 36(b) 37(c) 38(d) 39(d) 40(c) 41(c) 42(c) 43(c) 44(b) 45(d) 46(b) 47(d) 48(a) 49(c) 50(d) 51(d) 52(a) 53(d) 54(b) 55(c) 56(d) 57(a) 58(b) 59(d) 60(c) 61(a) 62(c) 63(b) 64(d) 65(b) 66(d) 67(d) 68(d) 69(d) 70(c) 71(d) 72(d) 73(b) 74(b) 75(b) 76(a) 77(a) 78(d) 79(b) 80(b) 81(c) 82(c) 83(c) 84(d) 85(b) 86(b) 87(a) 88(c) 89(c) 90(c) 91(b) 92(a) 93(b) 94(c) 95(a) 96(b) 97(d) 98(a) 99(a) 100(c) 101(c) 102(b) 103(c) 104(c) 105(a) 106(b) 107(d) 108(b) 109(b)

110(b) 111(a) 112(a) 113(b) 114(a) 115(d) 116(a) 117(c) 118(c) 119(c)
120(c) 121(c) 122(c) 123(a) 124(d) 125(c) 126(b) 127(b) 128(a) 129(a)
130(d) 131(a) 132(b) 133(b) 134(c) 135(b) 136(a) 137(c) 138(a) 139(a)
140(a) 141(d) 142(b) 143(d) 144(b) 145(c) 146(c) 147(d) 148(a) 149(a)
150(b) 151(d) 152(a) 153(a) 154(a) 155(b) 156(c) 157(b) 158(b) 159(b)
160(a) 161(c) 162(b) 163(d) 164(a) 165(d) 166(c) 167(a) 168(d) 169(c)
170(b) 171(a) 172(c) 173(b) 174(a) 175(d) 176(b) 177(d) 178(b) 179(b)
180(b) 181(c) 182(d) 183(b) 184(d) 185(a) 186(a) 187(b) 188(a) 189(b)
190(a) 191(d) 192(b) 193(a) 194(b) 195(a) 196(b) 197(b) 198(b) 199(a)
200(c) 201(b) 202(d) 203(a) 204(d) 205(b) 206(a) 207(a) 208(c) 209(b)
210(c) 211(b) 212(d) 213(c) 214(d) 215(c) 216(b) 217(d) 218(b) 219(d)
220(a) 221(b) 222(a) 223(d) 224(a) 225(d) 226(b) 227(a) 228(a) 229(b)
230(d) 231(a) 232(b) 233(a) 234(a) 235(b) 236(c) 237(b) 238(d) 239(b)
240(c) 241(c) 242(c) 243(a) 244(d) 245(b) 246(a) 247(b) 248(c) 249(b)
250(b) 251(c) 252(d) 253(a) 254(c) 255(b) 256(c) 257(b) 258(c) 259(b)
260(a) 261(a) 262(b) 263(a) 264(c) 265(a) 266(d) 267(d) 268(a) 269(a)
270(b) 271(b) 272(c) 273(c) 274(a) 275(b) 276(c) 277(a) 278(b) 279(b)
280(b) 281(b) 282(c) 283(a) 284(a) 285(b) 286(b) 287(c) 288(d) 289(d)
290(b) 291(b) 292(c) 293(a) 294(b) 295(c) 296(a) 297(b) 298(b) 299(b)
300(b) 301(b) 302(c) 303(c) 304(d) 305(b) 306(a) 307(c) 308(a) 309(b)
310(a) 311(b) 312(d) 313(a) 314(b) 315(b) 316(d) 317(c) 318(d) 319(d)
320(b) 321(a) 322(b) 323(a) 324(a) 325(a) 326(b) 327(d) 328(d) 329(d)
330(d) 331(c) 332(a) 333(d) 334(d) 335(c) 336(d) 337(d) 338(b) 339(d)
340(c) 341(c) 342(b) 343(a) 344(b) 345(b) 346(b) 347(c) 348(c) 349(c)
350(a) 351(d) 352(b) 353(a) 354(b) 355(c) 356(b) 357(b) 358(c) 359(d)
360(a) 361(c) 362(b) 363(a) 364(c) 365(d) 366(a) 367(b) 368(c) 369(a)
370(c) 371(b) 372(a) 373(a) 374(a) 375(b) 376(a) 377(c) 378(a) 379(d)
380(d) 381(d) 382(a) 383(a) 384(a) 385(b) 386(b) 387(a) 388(b) 389(b)
390(b) 391(b) 392(c) 393(c) 394(a) 395(a) 396(b) 397(c) 398(c) 399(a)
400(a) 401(a) 402(b) 403(a) 404(c) 405(d) 406(d) 407(c) 408(a) 409(a)
410(b) 411(b) 412(a) 413(d) 414(c) 415(c) 416(c) 417(c) 418(b) 419(b)
420(c) 421(d) 422(c) 423(c) 424(d) 425(d) 426(d) 427(d) 428(d) 429(b)
430(b) 431(d) 432(c) 433(d) 434(d) 435(d) 436(c) 437(c) 438(a) 439(c)
440(c) 441(c) 442(c) 443(d) 444(a) 445(c) 446(a) 447(b) 448(c) 449(a)
450(d) 451(b) 452(c) 453(a) 454(c) 455(b) 456(d) 457(c) 458(d) 459(c)
460(d) 461(c) 462(d) 463(c) 464(c) 465(c) 466(c) 467(b) 468(a) 469(a)
470(d) 471(c)

CHAPTER - 5

Soil Chemistry

1. Colloidal particles are usually smaller in diameter
   (a) 1 micrometer (b) 50 micrometer
   (c) 10 micrometer (d) 100 micrometers
2. The migration of colloidal particles under the influence of an electric field is called
   (a) Tyndall effect (b) Chemisorption
   (c) Electro-osmosis (d) Cataphorosis
3. Ion exchange phenomena was discovered by
   (a) Thompson & Way (b) Weighner
   (c) Adams & Holmes (d) Schofield
4. The Book 'Principle of Soil Chemistry' was written by
   (a) Russel (b) K.H.Tan
   (c) Adams (d) Oswall
5. 1 meq/100 g soil is equal to
   (a) 1 Cmol/kg (p+) (b) 100 Cmol/kg (p+)
   (c) 10 Cmol/kg (p+) (d) 50 Cmol/kg (p+)
6. Oxidation- reduction status of soil is measured as
   (a) pH (b) p^F
   (c) E_h (d) P^E
7. The end product of organic matter decomposition
   (a) Fulvic acid (b) Lignin
   (c) Humin (d) Humus
8. Father of Agriculture chemistry
   (a) Boussingault (b) Dokuchaev
   (c) Liebig (d) Jethrotull
9. DDT was first synthesized by
   (a) Arthur Young (b) Van Helmont
   (c) Paul Muller (d) M.S. Swaminathan

10. Theory of Humus Was explained during
    (a) 1809 (b) 1875
    (c) 1890 (d) 1820
11. What is the ionic radius of potassium
    (a) 1.33 Angstrom (b) 1.54 Angstrom
    (c) 0.98 Angstrom (d) 0.23 Angstrom
12. Avogadro's number is
    (a) 6×10^{23} (b) 6×10^{21}
    (c) 6×10^{23} (d) 6×10^{24}
13. The law of mass action was first reported by
    (a) Henderson (b) Guldberg and Waage
    (c) Jenny and Overstreet (d) Liebig
14. Lower size limit of soil colloid is
    (a) 20 angstrom (b) 100 angstrom
    (c) 50 angstrom (d) 10 angstrom
15. What is diameter of water molecules
    (a) 2 angstrom (b) 1 angstrom
    (c) 3 angstrom (d) 4 angstrom
16. The energy released when ions become hydrated is called as
    (a) Heat of Solution (b) Specific heat capacity
    (c) Heat of Wetting (d) Heat capacity
17. The energy released when clay become hydrated is called as
    (a) Heat of Solution (b) Specific heat capacity
    (c) Heat of Wetting (d) Heat capacity
18. It has higher CEC
    (a) FYM (b) Clay
    (c) Root (d) Humus
19. Sesquioxides are mostly oxides of
    (a) Sodium and calcium (b) Silicon and aluminum
    (c) Iron and aluminum (d) Silicon and sodium
20. Aluminum forms an octahedral shape by coordinating with how many oxygen?
    (a) 2 (b) 4
    (c) 6 (d) 8
21. Which is a characteristic of allophone clay?
    (a) It has a 1.1 crystal lattice (b) It has a 2.1 crystal lattice
    (c) It is a type of sesquioxide (d) It is amorphous volcanic clay

22. Young or only slightly leached soils are most likely to have which type of clay?
    (a) Motmorillonite (b) Kaolinite
    (c) Sesquioxide (d) Gibbsite
23. In a soil of moderate pH, which exchangeable cation nearly always dominates on exchange sites?
    (a) Sodium (b) Potassium
    (c) Calcium (d) Magnesium
24. Which is the preferred unit for expressing cation exchange capacity?
    (a) dS/m (b) cmole (p^+)/kg
    (c) mg/m^3 (d) Pascal
25. Which of the following minerals has the greatest cation exchange capacity?
    (a) Sand (b) Montmorillonite
    (c) Sesquioxide (d) Kaolinite
26. Which plant nutrient is always in cation form in both the soil and plant?
    (a) Nitrogen (b) Potassium
    (c) Sulfur (d) Chlorine
27. Comparing the concentration of H+ in a soil solution of pH 4 to that of a solution with pH 5, the pH 4 solution has
    (a) 20 percent more H^+ (b) 20 percent less H^+
    (c) 10 times more H^+ (d) 10 times less H^+
28. For determining basic cation saturation percentage, which cations are not considered be basic?
    (a) Ca^{2+} and Mg^{2+} (b) Na^+ and K
    (c) NH_4^+ and Na (d) $A1^{3+}$ and H^+
29. The so-called basic cations are actually which type of acid?
    (a) Lewis (b) Lowry-Bronsted
    (c) Organic (d) None of the above
30. Of the soil pairs below, which would be most buffered against changes in pH?
    (a) Sandy and rocky (b) Sandy and silty
    (c) Organic and clay (d) Loamy and silty
31. The structures of Il clay minerals are so-named because they contain
    (a) Two cations for every anion
    (b) Two negative charges for every positive charge
    (c) Two oxygens for every hydroxyl
    (d) Two tetrahedral layers for every octahedral layer

32. Isomorphous substitution creates net negative charges in clay micelles. A typical example of this process is the substitution of
    (a) Two Na ions for one Ca_2^+ion
    (b) An inner sphere complex for an outer sphere complex
    (c) One O_2^- for one OH^- in a tetrahedral
    (d) Mg^{2+} for Al^{3+} in an octahedral
33. Diffraction patterns made by X-rays are used to study colloid structures. For example, this technique is typically used to identify .... in soils.
    (a) Hunuic compounds (b) Allophane
    (c) Vermiculite (d) All of the above
34. Raising the soil pH from 5.0 to 6.5 using limestone would produce the greatest increase in "cation exchange capacity if the soil colloids were mainly............
    (a) Humus (b) Smectite
    (c) Kaolinite (d) Vermiculite
35. Which of the following soil pH levels indicates an alkaline soil?
    (a) pH 5.5
    (b) pH 6.5
    (c) pH = 7.5
    (d) Additional information is needed to answer
36. A soil pH of 3.0 would be typical of which of the following?
    (a) A humid region cropland soil
    (b) A humid region forest soil
    (c) An acid sulfate soil
    (d) A sodic soil
37. Crops grown on arid region soil commonly suffer from a deficiency of
    (a) Ca (b) Fe
    (c) K (d) Mg
38. A soil contains the following exchangeable cations in the indicated amounts. What is the percentage of acid saturation? Al^{3+} cmol (+), Ca^{2+} 3.5 cmol (t), $H^{=1}$ cmol (t), K^+ = 0.5 cmol (+), Mg^{2+} = 1.0 cm01 (+).
    (a) 11% (b) 33%
    (c) 44% (d) 55%
39. The maximum oxidation state shown by Mn is in
    (a) Mn^{2+} (b) MnO_2
    (c) MnO_4^{2-} (d) MnO_4

40. The insoluble fraction obtained from soil on extraction with dilute alkali is:
    (a) Humin (b) Humic acid
    (c) Folic acid (d) None of the above
41. Ratio law given by
    (a) Russel (b) Chapman
    (c) Stem (d) Schofield
42. Interveinal chiorosis, smalling and narrowing of new leaves and die back symptoms in guava is due to the deficiency of
    (a) Cu (b) Mn
    (c) Zn (d) Fe
43. In acid soil, phosphorous is fixed as
    (a) Calcium phosphate (b) Iron and Aluminium phosphate
    (c) Fluroapatite (d) Hydroxyapalite
44. Potassium fixation is higher in
    (a) 1:1 type clay (b) Oxide of Fe and Al
    (c) 2:1 type clay (d) None of the above
45. The cation which competes with ammonium during fixation is –
    (a) Aluminium (b) Magnesium
    (c) Potassium (d) None of the these
46. The principal cation that affect the availability fixation of phosphorus in alkali
    (a) Na and K (b) Fe and Al
    (c) Ca and Mg (d) None of the above
47. The acidity of H^+ absorbed on solid phase is known as
    (a) Reserve acidity (b) Active acidity
    (c) None of the above (d) Both of the above
48. The acidity of H^+ in aqueous phase of soils is called
    (a) Permanent charge (b) Reserve acidity
    (c) Active acidity (d) None of the above
49. Organic matter contains about ... percent organic carbon-
    (a) 18 (b) 68
    (c) 32 (d) 58
50. Per cent nitrogen is equal to
    (a) Per cent organic matter × 0.05
    (b) Per cent organic matter × 5
    (c) Per cent organic matter × 0.5
    (d) None of the above

51. The direct exchange of ions between the roots and clay colloids called
(a) Soil solution theory (b) Diffusion
(c) Contact exchange theory (d) None of the above
52. A decrease in redox potential below 0.2 V.
(a) Destroys nitrates
(b) Destroys NH4 and N-fixation
(c) Increase sulphur, zinc and copper availability
(d) Decrease phosphorus silicon, iron and manganese availability
53. A pH of 6.5-7.0 in soil solution regardless of pH before flooding
(a) Decrease phosphorus availability
(b) Favours nutrient absorption
(c) Checks organic matter mineralization
(d) No effect on nutrient absorption
54. The main steps in pyrite formation in acid sulphate soil area
(a) Oxidation of sulphate
(b) Reduction of hydrogen suiphide
(c) Dissolution of iron monosulphate
(d) None of these
55. Sodic soils contain sufficient..... to interfere with pant growth
(a) Exchangeable calcium (b) Exchangeable potassium
(c) Exchangeable sodium (d) Exchangeable magnesium
56. The roots of tomato and sunflower when in contrast of water table become
(a) Diageotrophic/negative geotropic
(b) Remain unaffected
(c) Positive geotropic
(d) Positively geotropic
57. In an anerobic soil root extension into anerobic and highly reduced layer is restricted injurious concentrations of
(a) Phosphorus (b) Iron
(c) Nitrogen (d) None of these
58. The bacteroid Rhizobium is
(a) Macroaerobic (b) Anerobic
(c) Microaerobic (d) None of these
59. Additional wall structures presume ably lignin/suberin in the aeranchymatous roots, in a waterlogged soil are formed in non-wetland plants namely
(a) Soybean (b) Groundnut
(c) Maize/sorghum/wheat/barley (d) Mungbean

60. The changes in plant cells membrane, lipid composition can modify
    (a) Fluidity (b) Alter permeability
    (c) Only one of these (d) Both of these
61. Flooding of soil grown plants shown
    (a) Enhancement in phosphorus in shoots
    (b) Promotes ion accumulation by shoots
    (c) Depression in N and k in shoots
    (d) None of these
62. In maize, gas filled lacunae can occupy up to 80 per cent of midcortex in aerenchyrnatous roots without an effect on transport to state of
    (a) Boron (b) Manganese
    (c) Potassium (d) Zinc
63. Rates of root fresh-weight increase close to maximal have been recorded at oxygen pressure of 0.001-0.05 atm. with
    (a) Sorghum (b) Tomato/tobacco/soybean
    (c) Safflower (d) Wheat
64. The diffusion of 150 from shoots to a point 15 cm along with a root has been detectable in
    (a) In both b and c
    (b) Aerenchymatous rice roots
    (c) Nonaerenchymatous barley roots
    (d) In none of these
65. Flooding in a wide range of plant species brings about
    (a) Rapid respiration (b) Rapid wilting
    (c) Rapid transpiration (d) Rapid nutrient absorption
66. The decreased root permeability in flooded plants is on account of concentration
    (a) Low hydrogen (b) Low oxygen
    (c) Low nitrogen (d) Red respiration
67. Zinc deficiency during early growth is caused by its immobilization in roots by carbonate ions soon after the submergence of soils
    (a) Acid (b) Saline-alkali
    (c) Alkaline (d) Saline
68. Iron toxicity can be ameliorated by
    (a) Continuous soil submergence
    (b) Application of P and N as urea
    (c) Application of lime and compost
    (d) All of these

69. Rice plants show no manganese induced toxicity symptoms up to its tissue level of
   (a) 6000 (b) 4000
   (c) 3000 (d) 5000
70. The diffusion coefficient of ethylene in water is less by .... folds than it is in the air
   (a) 20,000 (b) 15,000
   (c) 10,000 (d) 5,000
71. One of the most commonly observed morphological phenomena associated with water logging is the production of
   (a) Seminal roots (b) Adventitious roots
   (c) Crown roots (d) Tap roots
72. The status of soil oxygen may be characterized as a
   (a) Quantity factor (b) Intensity factor
   (c) Quality factor (d) None of these
73. Mean annual carbon dioxide concentration in the atmosphere currently is
   (a) 0.03 per cent (b) 0.02 per cent
   (c) 0.04 per cent (d) 0.05 per cent
74. Oxygen in the atmosphere is nearly constant is
   (a) 11 per cent (b) 31 per cent
   (c) 41 per cent (d) 21 per cent
75. Nitrogen in the ambient atmosphere is nearly constant at
   (a) 48 per cent (b) 68 per cent
   (c) 78 per cent (d) 58 per cent
76. Show poor germination under water
   (a) Maize (b) Celery
   (c) Bermuda grass (d) Lettuce
77. Good germination under water occurs in
   (a) Tomato (b) Buckwheat
   (c) Lettuce (d) Rice
78. Stem hypertrophy associated with hooding is caused by........
   (a) Interaction of ethylene and auxins auxins
   (b) Carbon dioxide and nitrogen
   (c) Interaction of zinc and manganese
   (d) Sulphate dioxide and oxygen
79. Flooding brings about the accumulation of in flooded tissues of sunflower
   (a) Indole acetic acid (b) Oxalic acid
   (c) Naphthalene acetic acid (d) Butyric acid

80. Adventitious water roots have been observed to occur in
    (a) Tomato (b) Okra
    (c) Gourds (d) Cucumber
81. The coleoptiles of .... serves an entry for oxygen to the germinating seed under water or in air –
    (a) Sunflower (b) Sorghum
    (c) Maize (d) Rice
82. Oxygen diffusion primarily in a number of woody species occurs through lenticels
    (a) Atmosphere (b) Lonosphere
    (c) Stratosphere (d) Rhizosphere
83. It has been assumed that the development of intercellular space in the cortex of rots provides pathway for oxygen diffusion in ....
    (a) Oats (b) Barley
    (c) Wheat (d) Buckwheat
84. Root anaerobiosis in tomato resulted in
    (a) Increase in glutamine
    (b) Decrease in alpha-aminobutyric acid
    (c) Increase in glutamic acid
    (d) Decrease in alanine
85. Very salt tolerant halophytes namely ....can survive and grow in salinities in excess of 500 mol m^3 sodium chloride
    (a) Vitis vinifera (b) Glycine max
    (c) Persea Americana (d) Saueda martima
86. Soil strength for engineering purposes is determined by the characteristics viz
    (a) Compactibility (b) Bearing resistance
    (c) Compressibility (d) All of these
87. Type of water vapour movement which occurs in soils is ....
    (a) External (b) Internal
    (c) Both of these (d) None of these
88. Capillary movement of water is complemented by
    (a) Leaf orientation (b) Stem elongation
    (c) Root extension (d) None of these
89. When a plant is under soil moisture stress, the roots
    (a) Shrink in size (b) Rot extension
    (c) Remain unaffected (d) None of these

90. Humus Colloids are composed basically of
(a) Carbon (b) Ozone
(c) Helium (d) Nitrogen

91. The most impotent silicate clays are known as ....
(a) Photosilicates (b) Autosilicates
(c) Simply silicates (d) Phyllosilicates

92. None humic substances are less complex and are . .. To microbial attack than those belonging to humic group
(a) More resistant (b) More susceptible
(c) Less resistant (d) Less susceptible

93. Humus enhances the mineral breakdown and increases the availability of some
(a) Anions (b) Cations
(c) Neutral ions (d) None of plants

94. Which of the following is harmful to the higher plants
(a) Phenol carboxylic acid (b) Dihydroxystearic
(c) Vanillic acid (d) All of these

95. Gypsum an amendment applied to alkali soils belongs to .... type
(a) Low solubility (b) Acid former
(c) Soluble Ca-salt (d) None of these

96. The choice of chemical amendment may be influenced by the required for reaction in the soil
(a) Time (b) Cost
(c) Quantity (d) Quality

97. Calcium chloride is probably the most readily available source of soluble calcium but seldom used due to
(a) High cost (b) Application problem
(c) Non availability (d) None of these

98. Among the fruits, lemon, apple, plum have been placed in the .... Salt tolerance group-
(a) Low (b) Medium
(c) High (d) None of these

99. Barley, rape and cotton are salt tolerant
(a) Low (b) Medium
(c) High (d) None of these

100. North-east monsoon causes rainfall in the south eastern part of the peninsular India during –
(a) November-December (b) May-June
(c) February-March (d) September-October

101. The anti-quality constituent in young seedling of forage sorghum is –
(a) Coumarins (b) Acetic acid
(c) Terpenes (d) Hydrocyanic acid

102. Soil organic matter has many remarkable effects and one of them is given below, identify the same –
(a) Increased plasticity (b) Enhanced cohesion
(c) Encouraged granulation (d) Low cation exchange

103. The C/N ratio in the organic matter of the furrow slice (upper 15 cm) of arable soils commonly ranges from
(a) 6:1 to 7:1 (b) 18:1 to 19.1
(c) 3:l to 4:1 (d) 8:l to l5:1

104. Which of the following rotations is likely to leave soil richer in organic matter - „
(a) Continuous oats (b) Maize-Oats-Clovers
(c) Continuous maize (d) Continuous sorghum

105. Ammonium and potassium ions are apparently just the right size to fit into the cavities between the crystal units of
(a) Montmorillonhte (b) Vermiculite
(c) Kaolinite (d) None of these

106. Ammonia present in the soil can be lost in significant quantities from
(a) Alkaline soils (b) Acid soils
(c) Both of these (d) None of these

107. Etridiazol and nitrapyrin .... Oxidation of ammonia o nitrate
(a) Maintains (b) Accelerates
(c) Inhibits (d) No effect

108. In soil where the negative charge is pH dependent, liming increases CEC which result. in an increased potassium by the soil colloids and …… in solution
(a) Increase (b) Decrease
(c) Little effect (d) None of these

109. The soils of zones can supply adequate potassium for many years even under irrigation –
(a) Humid (b) Arid
(c) Temperate (c) Sub tropical

110. The tropical soils high in hydrous oxides of Iron and aluminium embody Ti torrential rains
(a) Resistance (b) Susceptibility
(c) None of these (c) Both of these (a & b)

111. Soil brought by Ganga-Yamuna and Indus rivers and their tributaries are deep and are known as –
    (a) Bhabar soils (b) Alluvial soils
    (c) Vindhyan soils (d) Desert soils
112. The size of pesticide molecule, if all other conditions are constant, greatly influences it's
    (a) Absorption (b) Solubilizaion
    (c) Adsorption (d) Volatilization
113. Some pesticides with positively charged groups are also absorbed by
    (a) Illite clays (b) Montmorillonite
    (c) Kaolinite clays (d) Silicate clays
114. In general, herbicides are .... than either fungicides of insecticides
    (a) More mobile (b) More immobile
    (c) Equally mobile (d) Less mobile
115. Some degradation products of pesticides are even..... that the original pesticides
    (a) Equally toxic (b) Less toxic
    (c) Non-toxic (d) More toxic
116. The total number of bacteria frequently after fumigation –
    (a) Increases (b) Decreases
    (c) Remains constant (d) None of these
117. The process of ammonification is often by the use of pesticides
    (a) Harmed (b) Benefited
    (c) Not affected (d) None of these
118. The estimates postulate that the carbon dioxide content of atmosphere has increased from 280 parts per million to during last three decades-
    (a) 350 ppm (b) 400 ppm
    (c) 450 ppm (d) None of these
119. Nitrate levels in drinking water above about mg per liter are considered a human health hazard-
    (a) 10 (b) 15
    (c) 5 (d) 20
120. The discovey of oxygen was done by which proved the keystone of other discoveries that wet far toward unlocking the mystery of plant life –
    (a) John Mayow (b) John Woodward
    (c) Priestly (d) Banjamin Franklin

121. There was not only one "principle of vegetation" as reflected by agricultural writings during 17th nd 18th centuries was observed by
   (a) Francis Home (b) Guy Baird
   (c) 'William Michael (d) Jone Cummings
122. Groundnut is not an economical crop for deep black soils because
   (a) Phosphorus requirement is high
   (b) Swelling and shrinkage affect root system
   (c) Peg penetration is very poor
   (d) Peg penetration is very poor
123. The maximum carbon dioxide concentration at normal atmospheric levels occur low light intensities of foot candles for some plants –
   (a) 2500-5000 (b) 2150-2450
   (c) 1000-2000 (d) 6000-2000
124. Tomato plants grown on soils with low bulk densities of tended to be
   (a) High in anthocyanin (b) Low in protein
   (c) High in Sugar (d) Showed no effect
125. Cellulose is a –
   (a) Polysaccharide (b) Starch
   (c) Monosaccharide (d) Disaccharide
126. Chlorosis refers to the
   (a) Development of reddish brown colour on the leaf
   (b) Yellowing of the leaf tissues
   (c) Death of the leaf tissues
   (d) Burning of the leaf tissues
127. The cuticular membranes are generally more permeable to –
   (a) Cation rather than anions (b) Cations and anions both
   (c) Anions rather than cation (d) None of the above
128. Phosphorus fixation refers to the phenomenon of
   (a) Conversion of soluble phosphorus into plant unavailable forms
   (b) Absorption of phosphorus by the plant and synthesis of biological compounds
   (c) Leaching of phosphorus from soil by percolating waters
   (d) Anion exchange with colloidal constituents of soil
129. Which of the following is not a metamorphic rock?
   (a) Marble (b) Conglomerate schists
   (c) Quartzite (d) Stand stone

130. Kaolinite is a ... type clay mineral
(a) 3:1 (b) 2.2
(c) 1:1 (d) None of these

131. $Si_3Al_{10}(OH)_8$ is a formula of
(a) Muscovite (b) Kaolinite
(c) Mica (d) Biotite

132. C-spacing of Kaolinite is
(a) 7.39° A (b) 14.0° A
(c) 10.2° A (d) None of these

133. $Si_40_{10}(OH)sn\ H_20$ is a formula of
(a) Kaolinite (b) Muscovite
(c) Halloysite (d) Vermicultute

134. The C — spacing of Holloysite is –
(a) 14.0° A (b) 10.2°A
(c) 7.39° A (d) None of these

135. $K_2(Si_5\ Al_2)\ Al_4\ O_{20}\ (OH)_4$ is the formula of
(a) Muscovite (b) Biotite
(c) Kaolinite (d) Montmorillonite

136. Mica is .... type non expendable, K is present inside the layers
(a) 2:2 (b) 1:1
(c) 2:1 (d) None of these

137. The CEC of Mica is about
(a) 50 me/100 gm (b) 140 me/100 gm
(c) 10 me/100 gm (d) 100 me/100 gm

138. The CEC of illite is about –
(a) 40 me/100 gm (b) 140 me/100 gm
(c) 10 me/100 gm (d) 100 me/100 gm

139. Montmorillonite and Vermiculite are the type minerals
(a) 1:2 (b) 1:1
(c) 2:1 (d) None of these

140. The CEC value of montmorillonite is............ me/100g.
(a) 80-140 (b) 80-160
(c) 80-150 (d) 80-170

141. A unit of illite consists of-
(a) Potassium (b) Alumina
(c) Silica (d) All of the above

142. Consider the following statements, in paddy fertilizer application should be directed to the –
(a) Oxidized zone (b) Reduced zone
(c) Surface (d) None above

143. The amount of P in soil and soil solution that can exchange with orthophosphate in addition to soil as measured by plant growth in soil system, is termed as –
(a) L-value (b) E-value
(c) A-value (d) None of the these

144. Force (dynes) acting on the surface of water at
(a) Surface tension (b) Cohesion
(c) Adhesion (d) None of these

145. A unit of Kaolinite crystal lattice consists of silica and aluminium in the ratio of
(b) 1:3 (b) 1:3
(c) 2:1 (d) 1:1

146. The CEC value of illite is ... me/100g
(a) 10-30 (b) 10-20
(c) 10-40 (d) 20-30

147. The CEC value of kaolinite is ... me/100g
(a) 3-10 (b) 80-150
(c) 10-30 (d) None of these

148. A unit of Montmorillonite crystal lattice consists of silica and alumina in the ratio of
(a) 2:3 (b) 2:1
(c) 1:2 (d) 3:2

149. Soils with high pH are generally deficient in –
(a) Zn and Mn (b) Ca and Mg
(c) B and Fe (d) Cu and Mo

150. If the solution pH increases from 4 to 6, the H ion concentration decreases by
(a) 1/2 (b) 1/5
(c) 1/10 (d) 1/100

151. pH may be defined as
(a) Negative log of OH ion concentration
(b) Log of H ion concentration
(c) Negative log of H ion concentration
(d) Log of OH ion concentration

152. A value is given by
(a) Marshall (b) Frid and Dean
(c) Stevenson (d) Larsen

153. The phosphate potential is denoted as
(a) ½p Ca+pH_2PO_4 (b) pH - ½ p Ca
(c) R.T. in K^+/Ca^{++} (d) p Ca + pH_2PO_4

154. The unit of fertilizer or any other growth factor which is necessary to produce the yield which in 50% of 'maximum possible yield is called
(a) Fertilizer unit (b) Standard unit
(c) Optimum unit (d) Baule unit

155. Which of the following fertilizer has maximum plant nutrient –
(a) Murate of potash (b) DAP
(c) TSP (d) Ammonium nitrate

156. Process of immobilization refers to –
(a) Conversion of inorganic form to organic form
(b) Conversion of N-compotiflbs to protein
(c) Conversion of organic form to inorganic form ?
(d) None of the above

157. Ammonium sulphate contains ....
(a) 49% (b) 20%
(c) 42% (d) 46%

158. What is the P_2O_5 content of various rock phosphates
(a) 20-35% (b) 49%
(c) 11-20% (d) 18-20%

159. Which nutrient is maximum given for raising the field crops
(a) Nitrogen (b) Phosphorus
(c) Potash (d) Calcium

160. The fertilizers which have two or more than two major plant nutrient in their, chemical composition are called
(a) Complex fertilizer (b) Organic fertilizer
(c) Double fertilizer (d) Mixed fertilizer

161. The organic matter content of Indian peat and marshy soil is
(a) >10% (b) 10-40%
(c) >40% (d) None of the above

162. The availability of phosphorus is optimum in the pH range of –
(a) <7 (b) 6-8
(c) 54 (d) 7-8

163. Which of the following would one find in a submerged rice field?
(1) Reduced state
(2) Ammonical nitrogen
(3) Ferrous sulphide
(a) 3 alone (b) 1 & 3
(c) 1 alone (d) 1, 2 & 3

164. ....of the NH4′ in a region of alkaline. microsite helps to restore the conditions suitable for the normal conversion of NO_2^- to NO_3^-
(a) Dilution (b) Diffusion
(c) Both of these (d) None of these

165. The losses of ammonia usually become greater with
(a) Decrease in calcium (b) Decrease in temperature
(c) Decrease in soil pH (d) Increase in soil pH

166. The highest percentage content of nitrogen among the commonly used nitrogenous fertilizers is embodied by –
(a) Ammonium nitrate (b) Urea sulphate
(c) Urea (d) Anhydrous ammonia

167. Permissible biuret level in most of urea fertilizers is —— per cent –
(a) 4 (b) 2
(c) 3 (d) 5

168. In the fertilized soil with soil solution concentration of one ppm of phosphorus. mass flow contribution to phosphorus nutrition of crops could approach per cent –
(a) 40 (b) 0
(c) 30 (d) 20

169. The quantity of solid phase phosphorus that acts as reserve is often referred to as
(a) Intensity factor (b) Quality factor
(c) Quantity factor (d) None of these

170. Phosphate enzymes play a major role in of organic phosphates in soil –
(a) Immobilization (b) Mass transportation
(c) Mineralization (d) None of these

171. The mineralization of organic phosphorus lias been studied in relation to ratio
(a) C/N/S (b) C/N/P
(c) C/N/K (d) C/N/Ca

172. Clays such as kaolinite will fix larger quantities of phosphorus with SiO_2/R_2O_3 ratio
(a) High (b) Low
(c) Equal (d) None of these

173. Amorphous aluminosilicate minerals like allophone have .... negative charge which is partly or entirely balanced by complex alluminium cations
(a) Zero (b) Large
(c) Small (d) None of these
174. A minor portion of the phosphorus sorption capacity of soils originates from
(a) Sodium bicarbonate (b) Calcium carbonate
(c) Calcium oxide (d) Sodium carbonate
175. For each unit increase in pH, the concentration of Mn^{2+} decreased by folds
(a) 100 (b) 150
(c) 50 (d) 200
176. Use of phosphor-gypsum has been found to be useful in the amelioration of –
(a) Sub-soil acidity (b) Alkali soils
(c) Saline soils (d) Acid sulphate soils
177. Silica-sesquioxide ratio is useftil in the evaluation of sol in respect of –
(a) Silicon content (b) Nutrient availability
(c) Its age (d) Iron & aluminium content
178. Consider the following statements cation exchange of soil colloidal clay is due to –
(a) Silicon tetrahedrallayer (b) Hydration of clays
(c) Broken edges of clay lattices (d) Isomorphous substitution
179. Chlorites are basically silicates of
(a) Aluminium with some magnesium and aluminium
(b) Iron and Aluinium
(c) Magnesium with some iron and aluminium
(d) Iron with some magnesium and aluminium
180. The cation exchange capacity of a mineral soil containing predominately kaolinitic clay minerals generally ranges between-
(a) 80-100 me e per 10 gm. Soil
(b) More hen loo me. per 100 gm soil
(c) 3.15 m.e. per 100g soil
(d) 15-40 nie. per 100 gin soil
181. In soil science micelle stands for –
(a) Negatively charged silt particles with high CEC charge
(b) Colloidal panicle carrying positive charge
(c) Micropores in between textural particles change
(d) Colloidal particle carrying negative

182. In order to assess the immediate fertility level of a given soil for potassium, which one of he following forms of potassium present in soil would one test for?
    (a) Exchangeable K (b) K held in the silt
    (c) Water soluble K (d) Total K
183. X-ray different technique (s) is used to study –
    (a) Tracer studies (b) Photosynthesis
    (c) Clay mineralogy (d) None of these
184. At 1×10^{-9} H^+ concentration, what will be the pH value?
    (a) 6 (b) 10
    (c) 5 (d) 9
185. Anion exchange capacity is found minimum in the case of –
    (a) Motmorillonite (b) Kaolinite
    (c) Illite (d) None of these
186. Cation exchange capacity is found minimum in the case of
    (a) Motmorillonite (b) Humus
    (c) Illite (d) Kaolinite
187. The mineral chlorite has an extra layer of –
    (a) Brucite (b) Gibbsite
    (c) Montomorillonite (d) lute
188. Which one of the following minerals is the main source of boron in soil
    (a) Tourmaline (b) Hemimorphite
    (c) Haematite (d) Pyrolusite
189. Criteria of essentiality of nutrients or plants were given by –
    (a) Anion (b) Russed
    (c) Stout (d) Liebig
190. Appetite is a group of minerals which manly contains –
    (a) Sulphur (b) Titanium
    (c) Nitrogen (d) Phosphorus
191. The structural rigidity of kaolinite is due to –
    (a) K-bridge (b) H-bond
    (c) O-O bond (d) Internal absorbed water
192. A soil Formation process in which hums and sesquioxides become mobile and remain behind –
    (a) Calcification (b) Podsolization
    (c) Pedoturbation (d) Calcification
193. Attraction of slid surface for water molecule is called-
    (a) Adsorption (b) Adhesion
    (c) Cohesion (d) Absorption

194. Chlorite belongs to the
    (a) 2:2 type (b) 2:1 type
    (c) 1:1 type (d) Amorphous type
195. Montmorillonite is following type of clay mineral –
    (a) 2:2 (b) 3:1
    (c) 1: 1 (d) None of these
196. Soils are acidic for one of the reason
    (a) Acidic parent material (b) Basic slag
    (c) Low rainfall (d) None of these
197. A soil having pH 8.5 : ESP 15 and CE<4 dS/m′ at 25°C is known as –
    (a) Saline soil (b) Alkali soil
    (c) Recent alluvium (d) Saline alkali soil
198. A soil having pH 6.0 is called –
    (a) Acidic soil (b) Saline soil
    (c) Alkaline soil (d) Normal soil
199. The diameter of water molecule is approximately
    (a) 2.64° A (b) 2.54° A
    (c) 1.33° A (d) 2.940° A
200. How many order are included in the approximation system of soil classification –
    (a) 8 (b) 10
    (c) 12 (d) 15
201. Clay are classified as
    (a) Primary minerals (b) Hydroxy minerals
    (c) Secondary minerals (d) Tertiary minerals
202. Tolerance to sol salinity of the given set of crops is such that
    (a) Barley>Wheat>beans>uplands paddy paddy>beans
    (b) Barley>wheat>upland paddy> beans
    (c) wheat>barley>upland paddy>beans
    (d) wheat>barley>beans>upland paddy
203. Phosphorus fixation refers to the phenomenon of
    (a) Conversion of soluble phosphorus into plant unavailable forms
    (b) Absorption of phosphorus by the plant and synthesis of biological comp
    (c) Leaching of phosphorus from soil by percolating waters
    (d) Anion exchange with colloidal constituents of soil
204. Kaolinite is a ... type clay mineral
    (a) 3:1 (b) 2:2
    (c) 1:1 (d) None of these

205. $Si_4AI_{10}(OH)_8$ is a formula of

(a) Muscovite (b) Muscovite

(c) Mica (d) Vermiculture

206. C-spacing of Kaolinite is –

(a) 14.0° A (b) 14.0° A

(c) 10.2° (d) None of these

207. $Si4_0O10(OH)_8$ H_2O is a formula of

(a) Kaolinite (b) Muscovite

(c) Halloysite (d) Vermiculture

208. The C spacing of Holloysite is –

(a) 14.0° A (b) 10.2° A

(c) 7.39° A (d) None of these

209. $K_2(Si_5\ Al_2)$ Al4 O_{20} $(OH)_4$ is the formula of

(a) Muscovite (b) Biotite

(c) Kaolinite (d) Montmorillonite

210. Mica is .... type non expendable, K is present inside the layers

(a) 2:2 (b) 1:1

(c) 2:1 (d) None of these

211. The CEC of Mica is about

(a) 50 me/100 gm (b) 140 me/100 gm

(c) 10 me/100 gm (d) 100 me/100 gm

212. The CEC of illite is about –

(a) 40 me/100 gm (b) 140 me/100 gm

(c) 10 me/100 gm (d) 100 me/100 gm

213. Montniorillonite and Vermiculite are the type minerals

(a) 1:2 (b) 1:1

(c) 2:1 (d) None of these

214. A=B (1-Y) denotes A-value in which A is equal to –

(a) Amount of total nutrients in soil

(b) Amount of available nutrients in soil

(c) Amount of unavailable nutrients in soil

(d) None of the above

215. The CEC value of montmorillonite is.......... me/100 g

(a) 80-140 (b) 80-160

(c) 80-150 (d) 80-170

216. A unit of illite consists of

(a) Potassium (b) Alumina

(c) Silica (d) All of the above

217. Consider the following statements, in paddy fertilizer application should be direct the –
(a) Oxidized zone (b) Reduced zone
(c) Surface (d) None above

218. The amount of P in soil and soil solution that can exchange with orthophosphate in addition to soil as measured by plant growth in soil system. is termed as –
(a) L-value (b) E-value
(c) A-value (d) None of the these

219. Force (dynes) acting on the surface of water at right angle in one cm of length, is called-
(a) Surface tension (b) Cohesion
(c) Adhesion (d) None of these

220. Use of phosphor-gypsum has been found to be useful in the amelioration of –
(a) Sub-soil acidity (b) Alkali soils
(c) Saline soils (d) Acid sulphate soils

221. Silica-sesquioxide ratio is useful in the evalution of sol in respect of –
(a) Silicon content (b) Nutrient availability
(c) Its age (d) Iron & aluminium content

222. Consider the following statements cation exchange of colloidal clay is due to–
(a) Silicon tetrahedrallayer (b) Hydration of clays
(c) Broken edges of clay lattices (d) Isomorphous substitution

223. Anion exchange capacity is found minimum in the case of –
(a) Motmorillonite (b) Kolinite
(c) Illite (d) None of these

224. Cation exchange capacioty is found minimum in the case of –
(a) Motmorillonite (b) Humus
(c) Illite (d) Kolinite

225. Chemical weathering is governs mostly by the process –
(a) Hydrogen (b) Hydrolysis
(c) Carbonation (d) All of these

226. The systematic examination, description, classification and mapping of soil of an area is known as –
(a) Soil survey (b) Soil classification
(c) Soil mapping (d) All of above

227. All India Soil Survey and Land use Organization was established in -
(a) 1962 (b) 1050
(c) 1956 (d) 1960

228. The head office of All India Soil Survey and Land Use Organization is at -
(a) Madras (b) Bombay
(c) Nagpur (d) New Delhi

229. Which acts also as a nitrification inhibitor over and above a manure -
(a) Groundnut (b) Sesamum (Til)
(c) Neem (d) Groundnut

230. Which one of the following organic manures has the narrowest C/N ratio-
(a) Biogass slurry (b) Groundnut cake
(c) Farm yard manure (d) Compost

231. Biofertilizer is a –
(a) Mixture of inorganic fertilizer and microorganisms
(b) Mixture of organic manure and microorganisms
(c) Culture having he desired strain of microorganisms
(d) Decomposed compost enriched with mineral solubilizing bacteria

232. Super dieste3d compost is called so because –
(a) It contains plant nutrients more than that present in ordinary compost
(b) Superphosphate is added to he compost during its preparation
(c) It is prepared by allowing it to decompose beyond the normal process of decomposition
(d) Its P_2O_5 content is more than that present in the ordinary compost

233. The mineral chlorite has an extra layer of
(a) Brucite (b) Gibbsite
(c) Montomorillonite (d) Illite

234. Which one of the following minerals is the main source of boron in soil
(a) Tourmaline (b) Hemimorphite
(c) Haematite (d) Pyrolusite

235. Criteria of essentiality of nutrients or plants were given by -
(a) Arnon (b) Russed
(c) Stout (d) Liebig

236. Appetite is a group of minerals which mainly contains -
(a) Sulphur (b) Titanium
(c) Nitrogen (d) Phosphorus

237. The diagnostic horizon in Alfisol is termed -
(a) Spodic (b) Oxic
(c) Argillic (d) Mollic
238. Which of the following soils has got the highest bulk density -
(a) Clay Soil (b) Silty Soil
(c) Loam (d) Sandy Soil
239. The equation of soil formation, S=f(Cl, o, r, p, t) was given by -
(a) Glinka (b) Jenny
(c) Kellog (d) Dokuchaev
240. The structural rigidity of kaolinite is due to -
(a) K-bridge (b) H-bond
(c) O-O bond (d) Internal absorbewd water
241. A soil formation process in which hums and sesquioxides become mobile and remain behind -
(a) Clacification (b) Podsolization
(c) Pedoturbation (d) Calcification
242. Attraction of slid surface for water molecule is called -
(a) Adsorption (b) Addhesion
(c) Cohesion (d) Absortion
243. Erosion caused by spattering of sol particles by the impact of rain drops is known as -
(a) Sheet erosion (b) Gully eerosion
(c) Rill erosion (d) Splash erosion
244. Which of the following is not a metamorphic rock -
(a) Gneiss (b) Sandostone
(c) Lime stone (d) Conglomerate
245. Which of the following is not a sedimentary rock -
(a) Lime stone (b) Sandostone
(c) Congomerate (d) Gneiss
246. Chlorite belongs to the -
(a) 2:2 type (b) 2:1 type
(c) 1:1 type (d) Amorphous type
247. The soil layer of maximum leaching is indicated by the symbol -
(a) A_1 (b) A_2
(c) B_1 (d) B_2
248. The horizonswhich make up the profile of a lowest soil would include -
(a) A, C, & O (b) A, B, C, & O
(c) A, B, & C (d) B & O

249. National Remote Sensing Agency was established in -
(a) 1968 (b) 1977
(c) 1970 (d) Gneiss

250. The head quarter of NRSA is at -
(a) New Delhi (b) Secunderabad (Hyderabad)
(c) Bombay (d) Banglore

251. National Bureau of Soil Survey and Land Use Planning Head Quarter is at
(a) Culcutta (b) Nagpur
(c) Dehradun (d) Bombay

252. The diameter of the silt partical is
(a) 0.0005-0.0002 (b) 0.5 to 0.2 mm
(c) Less than 0.002 (d) 0.05-0.002

253. Different soil separate may be determined with the help of
(a) Yet's chart (b) Munsell chart
(c) International Pipety method (d) None of the above

254. The arrangement of small medium and large soil particles in set patterns is known as
(a) Mean weight diameter (b) Particle density
(c) Soil texture (d) Soil Structure

255. The natural soil aggregates are called as
(a) Soil separates (b) Mottling
(c) Peds (d) Concretion

256. The average soil bulk density of cultivated loamy soil is approximately
(a) 1.5-1.65 gm cm^{-3} (b) 1.1-1.4 gm cm^{-3}
(c) 1.5-1.0 gm cm^{-3} (d) None of these

257. The mass per unit volume of the solid mass of the soil excluding pore space is known as
(a) True density (b) Bulk density
(c) A and b both (d) None of these

258. A combination of many taxonomic unit likes oil series, phase or types is called
(a) Soil series (b) Soil complex
(c) Soil variant (d) Soil association

259. The patterns of occurrence of various soil taxonomic units on the detailed map is called
(a) Soil phase (b) Soil association
(c) Soil variant (d) Soil complex

260. The texture of surface soil of surface horizon is called
(a) Soil phase (b) Soil variant
(c) Soil series (d) Soil type

261. The characteristics of surface soil which have important bearing in soil management and crop production, is known as
(a) Soil phase (b) Soil series
(c) Soil variant (d) None of these

262. The representation of surface feature on mp and heir identification, is called
(a) Soil variant (b) Soil map
(c) Soil legend (d) None of these

263. An abrupt change in texture class of no continuity found between B and C horizon, is
(a) Lithological discontinuity (b) Regolith discontinuity
(c) Textural change (d) None of the above

264. How many times the soil organic matter hold the water of it is weight
(a) 20 times (b) 15 times
(c) 10 times (d) 25 times

265. Water drains by gravitational force from pores larger than
(a) About 30-60 micron (b) About 10-20 microns
(c) About 20-30microns (d) None of the above

266. Soils which high pH are generally deficient in
(a) Zn & Mn (b) Ca & Mg
(c) B & Fe (d) Cu & Mo

267. Which one of the following plant nutrients is useful in increasing resistance to diseases and insects-pests
(a) Calcium (b) Potassium
(c) Phosphorus (d) Nitrogen

268. Use of material like sulphur, poly form UF, isobutylidene diurea etc. improves fertilizer use efficiency. When such additives are used, the N- fertilizers are termed as
(a) Prilled urea
(b) Controlled release nitrogenous fertilizer
(c) Slow nitrifying N-fertilizer
(d) Complex fertilizer

269. Essential elements are those
(a) Which could be replaced by other elements with similar properties
(b) Which are required in large quantities
(c) Whose deficiency would prevent the completion of plant's like cycle
(d) Which would promote plant growth

270. Molybdenum is required by plants because it is a cofactor
    (a) Cytoihrome oxidase
    (b) Phosphatase
    (c) Nitrite Reductase
    (d) Nitrate reductase
271. Organic matter content of histosols' and hydromorphic soil is
    (a) 30-40%
    (b) 2-18%
    (c) 50-57%
    (d) 60-70%
272. The relative amounts of air & water in the pore spaces
    (a) Half filled and half empty
    (b) Always remain constant
    (c) Fluctuate continuously
    (d) All of the above
273. Moisture content from lower to upper plastic limit is known as
    (a) Stickly point
    (b) Plastic number
    (c) Field capacity
    (d) All the above
274. Soil colour determination is standardized and determined by the comparison of the soil colour to
    (a) Tensio meter
    (b) Munsell Chart
    (c) Gypsum block
    (d) None of these
275. "Hue" is the term which is used for determination of
    (a) Dominant spectral or rainbow
    (b) Relative thickness of whitness
    (c) Purity of the colour
    (d) All of the above
276. The main source heat energy for soil is
    (a) Infrared radiation
    (b) Solar radiation
    (c) Altra Violet radiation
    (d) None of the above
277. Specific heat of he mineral mater is
    (a) 1.0 cal gm^{-1}
    (b) 24.0 cal gm^{-1}
    (c) 0.462 cal gm^{-1}
    (d) 0.18 cal gm^{-1}
278. Example of cumulous material are
    (a) Gensiss
    (b) Till plain
    (c) Peat and Muck
    (d) Colluvial
279. Aeoline deposits are formed by the transportation of materials through
    (a) Wind
    (b) Sea
    (c) Running water
    (d) Ice
280. Solum is made up of
    (a) C horizon
    (b) C+ D horizon
    (c) A+B Horizon
    (d) C Horizon
281. Identify which of the following is a passive forming factors
    (a) Relief
    (b) Climate
    (c) Biosphere
    (d) None of these

282. Aridisol soils are found in the region of
   (a) Humid (b) Submerged
   (c) Arid (d) None of these
283. The dominant colour of spectral (rainbow) in soil indicate
   (a) Kaoline type of clay mineral (b) Value
   (c) Hue (d) Chroma
284. Montmorillonite is following type of clay mineral
   (a) 2:2 (b) 3:1
   (c) 1:1 (d) None of these
285. Soils are acidic for one of the reason
   (a) Acidic parent material (b) Basic Slag
   (c) Low rain fall (d) None of these
286. A Soil having pH 8.5, ESP 15 and CE<4 dsm-1 at 25oc is known as
   (a) Saline soil (b) Alkalie Soil
   (c) Recent alluvium (d) Saline alkali soil
287. A soil having pH 6.0 is called
   (a) Acidic soil (b) Saline soil
   (c) Alkaline soil (d) Normal soil
288. The diameter of water molecule is approximately
   (a) 2.64 A° (b) 2.54 A°
   (c) 1.33 A° (d) 2.94 o A°
289. How many order are included in the 7th approximation system of soil classification
   (a) 8 (b) 10
   (c) 12 (d) 15
290. Clay are classified as
   (a) Primary minerals (b) Hydroxy minerals
   (c) Secondary Minerals (d) Teritary minerals
291. Soils formed under impeded drainage condition where movement of air and water is restricted is known as
   (a) Acid Soil (b) Pozol
   (c) Gley Soil (d) Cheropzem
292. Physical weathering causes
   (a) Alternation of rocks and minerals
   (b) Decompositions rocks and minerals
   (c) Disintegration of rocks and minerals
   (d) Synthesis of rocks and minerals

293. Consider the following statements regarding the causes of low crop productivity of sandy soils
   (1) Sandy soils have very low water retention capacity
   (2) Applied plant nutrients easily leach out through drainage
   (3) Sandy soil have very low organic matter content
   (4) Sandy soil easily fix applied P. of these statements
   (a) 1, 2, & 3 are correct (b) 2, 3 & 4 are correct
   (c) 1, 2 & 4 are correct (d) 1, 3 & 4 correct
294. The phosphorous content as P in plough layer of one hectare of soil containing 0.1% P_2O_5 is
   (a) 430 kg (b) 860 kg
   (c) 1290 kg (d) 1500 kg
295. If the C:N ratio of crop residues is 20-30 than =
   (a) Mineralization may not take place
   (b) Immobilization may not take place
   (c) Immobilization may take place
   (d) All of these
296. If the C:N ratio of crop residue is more than 30 than
   (a) Partial mineralization will take place
   (b) Immobilization will take place
   (c) Mineralization will take place
   (d) All of these
297. If the C:N ratio of crop residues is less than 22, than
   (a) Mineralization will take place
   (b) Immobilization will take place
   (c) Both of these
   (d) None of these
298. The organism which can survive at the temperature 10-15° C is called
   (a) Psychrophylic (b) Mesophylic
   (c) Thremophilic (d) Thermiduric
299. The microbes which can survive at the temperature 25-30° is called
   (a) Thermoduric (b) Thermophilic
   (c) Mesophylic (d) Psychrophylic
300. Which nitrogenous fertilizer will you recommended for paddy crop
   (a) Nitrate fertilizer (b) Nitrate ammonical fertilizer
   (c) Amide fertilizer (d) All of the above

301. The common chemical preservatives are
(a) Calcium Chloride (b) Calcium sulphate
(c) Magnesium sulphate (d) None of the above
302. The average chemical composition of NPK percentage of night soil is
(a) 0.5-0.6-0.5 (b) 3.7-4.0-2.0
(c) 2.0-2.6-0.5 (d) 5.5-4.0-2.0
303. The residual effect of ammonical nitrogenous fertilizer in soil as
(a) Alkaline (b) Acidic
(c) Neutral (d) None of these
304. Urea is mineralized in the presence of enzyme
(a) Peptase (b) Urease
(c) Co-enzyme (d) All the above
305. When you apply 80 kg N/ha to wheat crop how many kg of urea would be required
(a) 12.00 kg (b) 80kg
(c) 173.91 kg (d) 100.25 kg
306. Single super phosphate (SSP) is manufactured from
(a) Rock phosphate (b) Bone meal
(c) Di-calcium phosphate (d) None of the above
307. Rhizobium leguminoserum can fix the nitrogen in the roots of
(a) Pea, sweet pea, lentil (b) Alfalfa, sweet clover
(c) Clovers (d) Beans
308. Rhizobium trifoli can fix the nitrogen in the roots of
(a) Sweet colour (b) Clover
(c) Soyabean (d) Lupines
309. Rhizobium species and the legume is called
(a) Non symbiotic N_2 fixation (b) Symbiotic N_2 fixation
(c) Both of these (d) None of these
310. Rhizobium phaseoli can fix the nitrogen in the roots of
(a) Soyabean (b) Pea
(c) Beans (d) Lentil
311. Rhizobium japonicum can fix the nitrogen in the roots of
(a) Soyabean (b) Cowpea
(c) Lentil (d) Beans
312. The N_2 fixation by Azospirillum in the cereals in called
(a) Non symbiotic N_2 fixation (b) Symbiotic N_2 fixation
(c) Both of these (d) None of these

313. Temperature has not significant effects on
(a) Structure (b) Weathering of rocks and minerals
(c) Biological activity (d) All of the above

314. Heterotrophic organic obtain energy from the biological oxidation of
(a) SO_4 (b) CO_2
(c) NH_4 (d) Organic carbon

315. Percentage of soil solids in soil is
(a) 50% (b) 40%
(c) 30% (d) 60%

316. Which of the following is known as fathe of pedology
(a) V.V. Dokuchaiev (b) D.G. Vilensky
(c) K.D. Glinka (d) C.F. Marbut

317. The average arable surface soil may be considered to have a particle density of about
(a) 3.00 gms/cc (b) 2.64 gms/cc
(c) 2.70 gms/cc (d) 3.00 gms/cc

318. The illuiviation is zone of
(a) Hard crust (b) Leaching
(c) Accumulation (d) None of these

319. The maximum moisture is available to plant at
(a) Wilting point (b) Hygroscopic coefficient
(c) Saturation (d) Field capacity

320. The method of survey adopted or intensive cultivation is
(a) Detailed survey
(b) Reonnaissance survey
(c) Detailed and reconnaissance
(d) All of the above

321. Soil air contain
(a) 2.5% CO_2 (b) 0.02% CO_2
(c) 3.0% CO_2 (d) 0.25% CO_2

322. The diagnostic surface horizons are called
(a) Polypedon (b) Pedon
(c) Epipedon (d) All of them

323. A thick dark coloured horizon which have high base saturation (50% or more) high organic matter content and with strong soil-structure, is called
(a) Ochric epipedon (b) Histic epipedon
(c) Umbric epipedon (d) Mollic epipedon

324. An epipedon which has dark colour low in base saturation is called
(a) Orchiric epipedon (b) Umbric epipedon
(c) Histric epipedon (d) Mollic epipedon
325. An man made epipedon which is similar to molic epipedon in many characters expect P_2O_5 content (more than 250 ppm) is
(a) Umbric epipedon (b) Anthtropic epipedon
(c) Orchric epipedon (d) Histic epipedon
326. Geological weathering takes place in
(a) Upper layers of soil (b) Lower layers of soil
(c) On earth crust (d) None of the above
327. Bone meal is well suited for
(a) Alkaline soil (b) Neutral soil
(c) Acidic soil (d) All of these
328. All potassium fertilizer's are physiologically alkaline, tere reaction with soil is
(a) Acidic (b) Alkaline
(c) Neutral (d) None of these
329. Which of the plant growth regulator is responsible for breaking dormancy
(a) Aluxin (b) Cytokinin
(c) Gibberellic acid (d) 2, 4-D
330. Papaya fruits are rich in the following
(a) Vitamin A (b) Vitamin D
(c) Vitamin E (d) Vitamin C
331. "Sugar Baby" is the variety of
(a) Muskmelon (b) Watermelon
(c) Pumpkin (d) Bittergourd
332. Maximum area under cashew-nut is in the state of
(a) West Bengal (b) Orissa
(c) Andhra Pradesh (d) Kerala

ANSWERS

1(a) 2(d) 3(a) 4(b) 5(a) 6(c) 7(d) 8(c) 9(c) 10(a) 11(a) 12(a) 13(b) 14(c) 15(c) 16(a) 17(c) 18(d) 19(c) 20(c) 21(d) 22(a) 23(c) 24(b) 25(b) 26(b) 27(c) 28(d) 29(a) 30(c) 31(d) 32(d) 33(c) 34(a) 35(c) 36(c) 37(b) 38(c) 39(c) 40(a) 41(d) 42(c) 43(b) 44(c) 45(c) 46(c) 47(a) 48(c) 49(d) 50(c) 51(c) 52(a) 53(b) 54(a) 55(c) 56(a) 57(b) 58(c) 59(c) 60(d) 61(c) 62(c) 63(b) 64(c) 65(b) 66(b) 67(c) 68(d) 69(c) 70(c) 71(b) 72(b) 73(a) 74(d)

75(c) 76(a) 77(d) 78(a) 79(a) 80(a) 81(d) 82(d) 83(b) 84(c) 85(d) 86(d)
87(c) 88(c) 89(a) 90(a) 91(d) 92(c) 93(b) 94(b) 95(c) 96(a) 97(a) 98(a)
99(c) 100(a) 101(d) 102(c) 103(d) 104(b) 105(b) 106(a) 107(c) 108(b) 109(c)
110(a) 111(b) 112(c) 113(d) 114(a) 115(d) 116(a) 117(b) 118(a) 119(a)
120(c) 121(b) 122(d) 123(c) 124(a) 125(a) 126(b) 127(a) 128(a) 129(d)
130(c) 131(d) 132(a) 133(c) 134(b) 135(a) 136(c) 137(a) 138(a) 139(c)
140(c) 141(d) 142(b) 143(a) 144(a) 145(d) 146(c) 147(a) 148(b) 149(b)
150(d) 151(c) 152(b) 153(a) 154(d) 155(b) 156(a) 157(b) 158(a) 159(a)
160(a) 161(b) 162(d) 163(d) 164(c) 165(d) 166(d) 167(b) 168(d) 169(c)
170(c) 171(b) 172(b) 173(b) 174(b) 175(a) 176(a) 177(d) 178(d) 179(a)
180(c) 181(d) 182(a) 183(c) 184(d) 185(b) 186(d) 187(a) 188(a) 189(a)
190(d) 191(b) 192(b) 193(b) 194(a) 195(d) 196(a) 197(b) 198(a) 199(a)
200(c) 201(c) 202(b) 203(a) 204(c) 205(d) 206(a) 207(c) 208(b) 209(a)
210(c) 211(a) 212(a) 213(c) 214(b) 215(c) 216(d) 217(b) 218(a) 219(a)
220(a) 221(d) 222(d) 223(b) 224(d) 225(d) 226(a) 227(c) 228(c) 229(c)
230(b) 231(c) 232(b) 233(a) 234(a) 235(a) 236(d) 237(c) 238(a) 239(b)
240(b) 241(b) 242(b) 243(c) 244(d) 245(d) 246(a) 247(b) 248(b) 249(a)
250(b) 251(b) 252(d) 253(c) 254(d) 255(c) 256(b) 257(a) 258(d) 259(d)
260(d) 261(a) 262(c) 263(a) 264(c) 265(a) 266(a) 267(b) 268(b) 269(c)
270(d) 271(d) 272(c) 273(b) 274(b) 275(a) 276(b) 277(d) 278(c) 279(a)
280(c) 281(a) 282(c) 283(c) 284(d) 285(a) 286(b) 287(a) 288(a) 289(c)
290(c) 291(c) 292(c) 293(a) 294(b) 295(b) 296(b) 297(a) 298(a) 299(c)
300(b) 301(b) 302(d) 303(b) 304(b) 305(c) 306(a) 307(a) 308(b) 309(b)
310(c) 311(a) 312(a) 313(a) 314(b) 315(a) 316(a) 317(b) 318(c) 319(d)
320(a) 321(b) 322(c) 323(d) 324(b) 325(b) 326(b) 327(c) 328(d) 329(b)
330(a) 331(c) 332(d)

CHAPTER - 6

Soil Microbiology

1. Phytophagous organisms do which of the following:
   (a) Extend root length (b) Fix nitrogen
   (c) Perform photosynthesis (d) Eat plant
2. With eutrophication the increased nutrient content normally causes a dramatic increase in populations of
   (a) Algae (b) Fungi
   (c) Virus (d) Frogs
3. The primary role of fungi and actinomycetes in the ecosystem is that of
   (a) Producer (b) Decomposer
   (c) Carnivore (d) Predator
4. The microbial decomposition of stockpiled organic materials into partially decomposed residues is called:
   (a) Activation (b) Allelopathy
   (c) Denaturing (d) Composting
5. Bacteria belong to the kingdom of living organisms known as:
   (a) Monera (b) Protista
   (c) Plantae (d) Fungi
6. The most common type of mycorrhizae is:
   (a) Rhizobium (b) VAM
   (c) Ectomvcorrhizae (d) Frankia
7. Organisms that derive their energy by ingesting reduced carbon are called:
   (a) Photoautotrophs (b) Chemoautotrophs
   (c) Heterotrophs (d) Mycoplasmas
8. What does nitrogenase do?
   (a) It lowers activation energy for dinitrogen fixation
   (b) It eats nitrogen
   (c) It creates nitrogen
   (d) It releases nitrogen into the atmosphere

9. Which actions encourage a healthy population of beneficial soil microbes?
   (a) Minimize soil sterilization or fumigation content
   (b) Maintain a high soil organic matter
   (c) Avoid drought
   (d) All the above
10. The word dirt evolved from ancient words that implied:
    (a) Death (b) Defecation
    (c) Disease (d) Dust
11. Humus is composed of which material[s]?
    (a) Humin (b) Fulvic acid
    (c) Humic acid (d) All the above
12. Which would be a typical decomposition product under anaerobic conditions?
    (a) SO_4 (b) H_2S
    (c) NO_3 (d) All the above
13. Which of the following may be considered soil "fauna"?
    (a) A nematode (b) A prairie
    (c) Amite (d) All the above
14. 'Azolla' (a nitrogen fixing organism) is in symbiotic association with –
    (a) Bryophyte and blue green algae
    (b) Fern and blue green algae
    (c) Nostac and blue green algae
    (d) Fungi and blue green algae
15. Paddy crop can be successfully grown under water logged conditions because
    (a) Paddy roots do not require O_2
    (b) Needed O_2 is supplied from the foliar parts of paddy to the roots
    (c) Paddy roots have capacity to absorb atmospheric O_2 directly
    (d) Needed O_2 is supplied by the microorganisms present in the soil
16. Sunflower oil is rated as good quality oil because it contains
    (a) Low quantity of unsaturated fatty acids
    (b) High quantity of saturated fatty acids
    (c) Low quantity of saturated fatty acids
    (d) High quantity of unsaturated fatty acid
17. What is the form in which zinc is absorbed by the plants
    (a) Zn (b) Zn^{++}
    (c) Zn (d) None

18. Which group of microbes increases phosphate solubility
    (a) Azotobacter (b) Rhizobium
    (c) Pseudomonas (d) Clostndium
19. Main objective of pudding in paddy is to
    (a) Destroy insect pests
    (b) Mix the fertilizer in the soil
    (c) Create impermeable layer is the soil
    (d) None is true
20. Potato is propagated through
    (a) Tuber
    (b) TPS (true potato seed)
    (c) Micro-tuber
    (d) All of these
21. Ammonia is converted into nitrate by
    (a) Fungus (b) Algae
    (c) Earthworms (d) Bacteria
22. Bacteria actinomycetes, fungi and algae are called as
    (a) Microfauna (b) Microflora
    (c) Macroflora (d) Macrofauna
23. Nitrification is mainly carried out by
    (a) Heterotrophic organism
    (b) Photoauto-tropic organism
    (c) Chemoautotrophic organism
    (d) Equal by different groups in general
24. Rhizobia infects the host legume through
    (a) Epidermal cells (b) Cortex cell
    (c) Root hairs (d) All the above
25. Rhizobium after infection converts to a form, which is irregular in shape and, is
    (a) Spore (b) Bacteria
    (c) Cyst (d) All the above
26. Oxidation of sulphur to sulphate is carried out by
    (a) Aspergithis spp. (b) Bacillus spp
    (c) Thiobacillus spp. (d) Azotobacter spp.

27. Release of nutrients like nitrogen, phosphorus or sulphur from the added organic matter by Microorganism at the initial stage of degradation will depend upon
    (a) Soil pH
    (b) Chemical composition of added organic matter
    (c) Soil temperature
    (d) Method of incorporation
28. Commonly used method for enumeration of soil microbial population is
    (a) Contact slide technique (b) Microscopic count
    (c) Microbial respiration (d) Dilution plate technique
29. Berseem seeds are inoculated with
    (a) Rhizobium culture (b) Azotobacter culture
    (c) Azolla culture (d) None of these
30. Father of soil microbiology is
    (a) Bejjenink (b) A.Waksman
    (c) S.N. Winogradsky (d) Liebig
31. Bacteria present in the root nodules of legume plants is
    (a) Clostridium (b) Rhizobium
    (c) Azotobactor (d) Azospirlium
32. The species of Rhizobium present in the root nodules of soybean is
    (a) R. leguminoosaruin (b) R. phaseoli
    (c) R. trifoli (d) R. japonicum
33. Blue green algae fix nitrogen mainly in
    (a) Rice fields (b) Sugarcane
    (c) Legumes (d) Cereals
34. Rhizosphere refers to the small area
    (a) On the root (b) Around the root
    (c) Near the primary root (d) All of the above
35. Mineralization of nitrogen refers to the conversion of
    (a) Inorganic form into organic form
    (b) Organic form to nitrogenous compound
    (c) Organic from into inorganic from
    (d) All of the above
36. The conversion of ammonia into nitrate by microorganisms is known as
    (a) Nitrification (b) Nitrogen fixation
    (c) Denitrification (d) Loss of nitrogen

37. The term adsorption means
    (a) Broken from surface (b) Adhere on surface
    (c) Separated from surface (d) a and b both
38. Reclamation of acidic soils increases pH with the use of
    (a) Gypsum (b) $Ca(OH)_2$
    (c) $CaSO_4$ (d) Pyrites
39. All potassium fertilizers are physiologically neutral there reaction with soils is
    (a) Acidic (b) Alkaline
    (c) Neutral (d) None of the above
40. Mycorrhyzea is a
    (a) Fungus + higher root plants (b) Bacteria + Fungus
    (c) Algae higher rot plants (d) None of the above
41. In CAN nitrogen is present in following from
    (a) Ammonical form (b) Nitrate
    (c) Both a and b (d) None of these
42. When you apply 80 kg. N/ha to heat crop, how may kg of urea would be required
    (a) 173.91 kg (b) 120.00 kg
    (c) 100.25 kg (d) 120.00 kg
43. The term nicotine means
    (a) Biopesticide (b) Insecticides
    (c) Only pesticides (d) Weedicides
44. High salt tolerance crop is
    (a) Bajra (b) Maize
    (c) Wheat (d) Barley
45. Natric origin is rich in
    (a) Calcium (b) Sodium
    (c) Potassium (d) None of the above
46. The temperature increase with increase in height in the phase of
    (a) Lithosphere (b) Tropospere
    (c) Inosphere (d) Atmosphere
47. Who has discovered the plant hormone gibreline
    (a) Skoog (b) F.W. Went
    (c) Kurosawa (d) Kogl
48. Ammonia is transformed into nitrate by:
    (a) Fungi (b) Algae
    (c) Bacteria (d) Actinomycetes

49. B1ue green algae grows best in flooded soils exposed to sun and occupied by
    (a) Sorghum (b) Rice crop
    (c) Jute crop (d) Sunhemp
50. Diatoms are
    (a) Minerals (b) Parent rocks
    (c) Soil bacteria (d) Soil algae
51. Maximum population of micro-organisms found
    (a) Bacteria (b) Fungi
    (c) Viruses (d) Actinomycetes
52. Fungal population is comparatively high in a soil having
    (a) Alkaline pH (b) Acidic to neutral pH
    (c) Acidic pH (d) Neutral pH
53. Fraction of organic matter comparatively resistant to microbial degradation is
    (a) Protein (b) Cellulose
    (c) Lignin (d) Hemi-Cellulose
54. Nitrification in the soil takes place by
    (a) Oxidation process
    (b) Biological oxidation
    (c) Reduction process
    (d) Both oxidation and reduction process
55. Dominant organisms found in a compost pit area
    (a) Thermophilic (b) Psychrophilic
    (c) Mesophilic (d) Psychrophilic and mesophilic
56. Organisms used as bio fertilizer in wheat cultivation
    (a) Azotohacer spp. (b) Rhizobium
    (c) a & b both (d) None of these
57. Among the soil fauna most abundant are
    (a) Nematodes (b) Protozoans
    (c) Both the of above (d) None of the above
58. System of naming microorganisms is known as
    (a) Hierarchical system (b) Binomial system
    (c) Adenosine system (d) None of the above
59. The term ecology means
    (a) The study of micro-organisms
    (b) The study of bacteria
    (c) The study of environment and Microorganisms
    (d) None of the above

60. Which one of the following microorganisms is involved in nitrification in the soil
(a) Micrococcus (b) Thiobacillus
(c) Pseudomonas (d) Nitrosomonas
61. Organic matter content under well-drained conditions is higher under
(a) Field. crops (b) Grasslands
(c) Forest covers (d) Fruit crops
62. The .... oxidation of ammonia has been termed as nitrification
(a) Biological (b) Chemical
(c) Physical (d) Physico-chemical
63. .... is considered to be most important of the soil organisms bringing about the conversion of NH_4^+ to NO_2^-
(a) Azotobacter (b) Azospilrillum
(c) Nitrobacter (d) Nitrosomonas
64. The rapid increase in denitrification at the elevated soil temperatures suggests that microorganisms play a major role in denitrification
(a) Cherhophilic (b) Photophilic
(c) Hydrophilic (d) Thermophilic
65. The earth worm casts care definitely higher in than the soil
(a) Bacteria (b) Organic matter
(c) Available nutrients (d) All of these
66. Development of acid soils in humid areas is Largely associated with
(a) Intense weathering
(b) Leaching out of basic cations
(c) Oxidation of pyrite
(d) Use of poor quality irrigation water
67. The crop plants transpire more when there is
(a) High temperature and low
(b) High humidity, and high wind velocity humidity
(c) High temperature and high humidity
(d) Low temperature and low humidity
68. An organism which converts nitrite to Nitrate is
(a) Azotobactor (b) Nitrobacter
(c) Nitrosomonas (d) Nitrogenase
69. The fundamental role of root hairs in plants is
(a) To absorb water and mineral salts from the Soil
(b) To bind soil particles to the root for firm fixation o the plant
(c) To product the young root from damage by coarse soil particles
(d) To protect he root from soil microbes

70. Water and mineral salts are translocated in plants in the
    (a) Xylem (b) Phloem
    (c) Collenchyma (d) Porenchymal, 2 & 4
71. Which one of the following micro-organisms is responsible for maximum nutrient cycling in the soil?
    (a) Fungi (b) Actinomycetes
    (c) Bacteria (d) Algae
72. When organic matter with wide C:N ratio (70:1) is added to the soil, the net effect is the disappearance of mineral nitrogen due to
    (a) Mineralization (b) Nitrogen reduction
    (c) Immobilization (d) Nitrogen transformation
73. What culture should be given priority on groundnut cultivation
    (a) Azospirilla (b) Rhizobia
    (c) Mycorrhiza (d) Frankia
74. Which fraction of humus is soluble both in alkali and alcohol?
    (a) Fluric acid (b) Humic acid
    (e) Hymaomelanic acid (d) Humin
75. Which crop has the maximum nitrogen fixing potential
    (a) Pigeon pea (b) Soybean
    (c) Guar (d) Groundnut
76. Rhizobium inoculation is effective only when an active and efficient strain is used under optimum-
    (a) FC (b) N
    (c) pH (d) Zn
77. If the nitrogen content of a soil is 0.56% the organic matter (%)
    (a) 5.6 (b) 0.95
    (c) 9.5 (d) 1.72
78. Which one of the following actinomycetes is responsible for N-fixation
    (a) Anabaena (b) Frankia
    (c) Clostridum (d) Azolla
79. In photosynthesis oxygen is liberated due to
    (a) Breakdown (b) Reduction of CO_2
    (c) Oxidation of 11:0 (d) Breakdown of chlorophyll
80. The plants which manufacture their own food in presence of light are known as
    (a) Photoautotroph (b) Phototropic
    (c) Autotropic (d) Photophytic

81. Photosynthesis does not take place in fungi due to absence of
(a) Chlorophyll (b) Potassium
(c) Nitrogen (d) Phosphorus
82. Zinc, Iron. Copper, Manganese and molybdenum are called micronutrients because they are
(a) Nutrients which produce microscopic effects
(b) Essential nutrients but are required in minute quantifies
(c) Nutrients required by micro-organisms
(d) Nutrients of microscopic significance
83. Symbiotic nitrogen fixation in Cajanus cajan (tur/arhar) madiated by
(a) Rhizobium spp (cowpea Rizo.) (b) Rhizobium phaseli
(c) Rhizobium lupine (d) Rhizobium leguminosarum
84. The ionic form of phosphorus is determined by pH of the solution. At pH 4.0 the predominated ionic forms of phosphorus, present are –
(a) H_2PO_4 (b) $H_2PO_4^{-1}$and PO_4
(c) HPO_4 (d) $H_2PO_4^{-1}$ and HPO_4^{-1}
85. Which acts also as a nitrification inhibitor over and above a manure
(a) Groundnut (b) Sesamum (Tu)
(c) Neem (d) Groundnut
86. Which one of the following organic manures has the narrowest C/N ratio
(a) Biogass slurry (b) Groundnut cake
(c) Farm yard manure (d) Compost
87. Biofertilizer is a
(a) Mixture of inorganic fertilizer and microorganisms
(b) Mixture of organic manure and microorganisms
(c) Culture having the desired strain of microorganisms
(d) Decomposed compost enriched with mineral solubilizing bacteria
88. Super digested compost is called so because
(a) It contains plant nutrients more than that present in ordinary compost.
(b) Superphosphate is added to the compost during its preparation
(c) It is prepared by allowing it to decompose beyond the normal process of decomposition.
(d) Its P_2O_5 content is more than that present in the ordinary compost.
89. How many times the soil organic matter hold the water of it is weight
(a) 20 times (b) 15 times
(c) 10 times (d) 25 times

90. The phosphorus content as P in plough layer of one hectare of soil containing 0.1% P_2O_5 is –
    (a) 430 kg (b) 860 kg
    (c) 1290 kg (d) 1500 kg
91. If the C:N ratio of crop residues is 20 30 than
    (a) Mineralization ma not take pla
    (b) Immobilization may not take place
    (c) Immobilizion may take place
    (d) Not known
92. IF the C:N ratio of crop residue is more than 30 than
    (a) Partial mineralization will take place
    (b) Immobilization will take place
    (c) Mineralization will take place
    (d) All of these
93. If the C:N ratio of crop residues is less than 22, than
    (a) Mineralization will take place
    (b) Immobilization will take place
    (c) Both of these
    (d) None of these
94. The organism which can survive at the temperature 10-15° C is called
    (a) Psychrophylic (b) Mesophylic
    (c) Thremophilic (d) Thermiduric
95. The microbes which can survive at the temperature 25 -30° C is called
    (a) Thermoduric (b) Thermophilic
    (c) Mesophylic (d) Psychrophylic
96. Which nitrogenous fertilizer will you recommend for paddy crop
    (a) Nitrate fertilizer (b) Nitrate ammoical fertilizer
    (c) Amide fertilizer (d) All of the above'
97. The common chemical preservatives are
    (a) Calcium chloride (b) Calcium sulphate
    (c) Mangnesium sulphate (d) None of the above
98. Rhizobium leguminoserum can fix the nitrogen in the roots of
    (a) Pea, sweet pea, lentil (b) Alfalfa.Sweet clover
    (c) Clovers (d) Beans
99. Rhizobiu trifoli can fix the nitrogen in the roots of
    (a) Sweet colour (b) Clover
    (c) Soyabean (d) Lupines

100. Rhizobium species and the legume is called
    (a) Non symbiotic N_2 fixation (b) Symbiotic N_2 fixation
    (c) Both of these (d) None of the above
101. Rhizobium phaseoli can fix the nitrogen in the roots of
    (a) Soybean (b) Pea
    (c) Beans (d) Lentil
102. Rhizobium japonicum can fix the nitrogen in the roots of
    (a) Soybean (b) Cowpea
    (c) Lentil (d) Beans
103. The N_2 fixation b Azotobacter and Azospirillum in the cereals in called
    (a) Non symbiotic N_2 fixation (b) Symbiotic N_2 fixation
    (c) Both of these (d) None of above
104. Heterotrophic organic obtain energy from the biological oxidation of
    (a) SO_4^{-2} (b) CO_2
    (c) NF_4^+ (d) Organic carbon
105. Biological nitrogen fixation is:
    (a) Both aerobic and anaerobic process
    (b) Aerobic process
    (c) Anaerobic process
    (d) None of above
106. Efficiency of symbiotic biological nitrogen fixation depends on
    (a) Ecological condition (b) Host characteristics
    (c) Microbial strain characteristics (d) All of the above
107. Denitrification is more in:
    (a) Well drained soils (b) Waterlogged soils
    (c) Heavy soils (d) Light soils
108. Organic matter influences water holding capacity of soil in the following manner
    (a) Is not affected at all (b) Is stabilized
    (c) Is decreased (d) Is increased
109. Accumulation of carbon dioxide which is at an especially high level when rice plants are vigorously growing has the following effect on blue green algae:
    (a) The algae produces phytotoxic metabolites
    (b) Nitrogen-fixation by the algae is reduced
    (c) N_{2-} fixation by the algae is enhanced
    (d) The algae growth is inhabited

110. Blue green algae grows best in flooded soils exposed to sun and occupied by
    (a) Sorghum (b) Rice crop
    (c) Jute crop (d) Sunhemp
111. Diatoms are
    (a) Minerals (b) Parent rocks
    (c) Soil bacteria (d) Soil algae
112. Maximum population of micro-organisms found in soils are
    (a) Bacteria (b) Fungi
    (c) Viruses (d) Actinomvcetes
113. Fungal population is comparatively high in a soil having
    (a) Alkaline pH (b) Acidic to neutral pH
    (c) Acidic pH (d) Neutral pH
114. Fraction of organic matter comparatively resistant to microbial degradation is
    (a) Protein (b) Cellulose
    (c) Lignin (d) Hemi-cellulose
115. Nitrification in the soil takes place b
    (a) Oxidation process
    (b) Biological oxidation
    (c) Reduction process
    (d) Both oxidation and reduction process
116. Dominant organisms found in a compost pit are
    (a) Thermophilic (b) Psychrophilic
    (c) Mesophitic (d) Psychrophilic and mesophilic
117. Organisms used as bio fertilizer in wheat cultivation
    (a) Azotobacer spp. (b) Rhizobium spp.
    (c) a & b both (d) None of these
118. There is a net increase in the mineralization of organic nitrogen in soil when
    (a) C:N = 20:1
    (b) C:N=20-30:1
    (c) C:N = 30: L
    (d) Nitrogen is taken up by the crops
119. The ratio of organic carbon to organic matter in soils is
    (a) 1.0:1.7 (b) 20.0:1.0
    (c) 1.0:2.0 (d) 1.7:1.0

120. Humus soil contains carbon oxygen nitrogen, hydrogen and ash in the ratio of

(a) 10:7:1:1:1 (b) 1:7:10:1:1

(c) 7:10:1:1:1 (d) None of the above

121. Humus soil contains carbon ...

(a) 5 (b) 35

(c) 50 (d) 5

ANSWERS

1(d) 2(a) 3(b) 4(d) 5(a) 6(b) 7(c) 8(a) 9(d) 10(b) 11(d) 12(b) 13(d) 14(b) 15(b) 16(d) 17(b) 18(c) 19(c) 20(d) 21(d) 22(b) 23(c) 24(c) 25(c) 26(c) 27(b) 28(d) 29(a) 30(c) 31(b) 32(d) 33(a) 34(b) 35(c) 36(a) 37(b) 38(b) 39(c) 40(a) 41(c) 42(a) 43(a) 44(d) 45(b) 46(b) 47(d) 48(c) 49(b) 50(d) 51(a) 52(c) 53(c) 54(b) 55(c) 56(a) 57(b) 58(b) 59(c) 60(d) 61(b) 62(a) 63(d) 64(d) 65(d) 66(b) 67(a) 68(b) 69(a) 70(a) 71(c) 72(c) 73(b) 74(b) 75(c) 76(c) 77(c) 78(b) 79(c) 80(a) 81(a) 82(b) 83(d) 84(a) 85(c) 86(b) 87(c) 88(b) 89(c) 90(b) 91(b) 92(b) 93(a) 94(a) 95(c) 96(b) 97(b) 98(a) 99(b) 100(b) 101(c) 102(a) 103(a) 104(b) 105(a) 106(d) 107(b) 108(d) 109(a) 110(b) 111(d) 112(a) 113(c) 114(c) 115(b) 116(c) 117(a) 118(b) 119(a) 120(a) 121(c)

CHAPTER - 7

Problematic Soil

1. Method used for the determination of lime requirement of an acid soil is
   (a) Moh'r method (b) Shoemaker's method
   (c) Olsen's method (d) Kieinaj's method
2. Which is not a major cause of soil acidity?
   (a) Carbon dioxide dissolved in rain
   (b) Use of phosphate fertilizers
   (c) Use of ammonium fertilizers
   (d) Excretion of H^+ by plant roots
3. Burned limestone (Cao) is also known as:
   (a) Slaked lime (b) Blast furnace slag
   (c) Marl (d) Quicklime
4. Which element becomes more available as pH decreases?
   (a) Manganese (b) Molybdenum
   (c) Calcium (d) All of the above
5. Ammonium reacts in soil to produce nitrate, water and
   (a) Aluminum (b) H^+
   (c) 0_2 (d) OH^+
6. Which material below is not a liming material?
   (a) Gypsum (b) Chalk
   (c) Marl (d) Oyster shells
7. Lime reacts in soil to produce carbon dioxide and
   (a) H^+ (b) O_2
   (c) H_2O (d) None of the above
8. Which aluminum species dominates at very low pH values, such as pH 4?
   (a) $A1[OH]^{3+}$ (b) $A1[OH]^{2+}$
   (c) $Al[OH]^2+$ (d) Al^{3+}

9. Which is not an essential component for the reclamation of sodic soil?
   (a) Adequate internal drainage (b) Proper tillage
   (c) Replacement of excess sodium (d) Leaching of excess salts
10. Which of the factors below contribute to soil salinity?
    (a) Shallow groundwater (b) Irrigation
    (c) Fertilizer (d) All the above
11. Which component of water potential can be estimated from measurements of soluble salts?
    (a) Osmotic (b) Matric
    (c) Pressure (d) Gravitational
12. Which fruit crop is most sensitive to salt?
    (a) Pate palm (b) Grape
    (c) Strawberry (c) Fig
13. When using the SAR formula in which units are concentrations of cations expressed?
    (a) dS/m (b) cmolc/kg
    (c) mol/L (d) me/L
14. EC of water added ÷ EC of drainage water is one formula for:
    (a) SAR (b) Leaching fraction
    (c) Evapotrenspiration (d) Gypsum requirement
15. In reclaiming sodic soils, the sodium in the soil colloids is changed with
    (a) Ammonium (b) Potassium
    (c) Hydrogen (d) Calcium
16. Which element commonly found in irrigation water can be toxic to plants?
    (a) Boron (b) Sodium
    (c) Chlorine (d) All the above
17. Which plants can tolerate seawater?
    (a) Mangrove (b) Salicornia
    (c) Asian wild rice (d) All the above
18. Which term describes "salt — loving "plants or plants that can tolerate high levels of salt?
    (a) Saliphytes (b) Halophytes
    (c) Xerophytes (d) Sodiphytes
19. When calculating the amount of irrigation water to apply to a crop to provide sufficient leaching which factor enters into the formula?
    (a) Texture (b) ESP of the soil
    (c) Salt tolerance of the crop (d) SAR of the water

20. Water erosion is distinguished by
    (a) Sheet erosion (b) Kill erosion
    (c) Gully erosion (d) All the above
21. Soil erosion by water is influenced greatly by
    (a) Precipitation (its intensity and amount
    (b) The type of soil
    (c) The slope of land (its degree and length)
    (d) The nature of the ground cover and land use
22. The area under alluvial soil affected by salinity and alkalinity in India is
    (a) 6.9 m ha (b) 8.9 m ha.
    (c) 10.5 m. ha (d) 7.9 m ha.
23. The process responsible for the formation of sodic soil is
    (a) Stalinization (b) Calcification
    (c) Podsolization (d) Alkalization
24. The harmful effect of saline soil is due to
    (a) Low osmotic pressure of soil solution
    (b) High pH
    (c) Low pH
    (d) High osmotic pressure of soil solution
25. The saline soil can be managed by
    (a) Addition of lime (b) Addition of pyrite
    (c) Addition of gypsum (d) Leaching of salts
26. Which or the following is connect explanation of ESP
    (a) $\frac{\text{Exch.Na}}{\text{CEC}}$ (b) $\frac{\text{Exch.Na}}{\text{CEC}} \times 100$
    (c) Exch.Na × 100 (d) $\frac{\text{CEC}}{\text{Exch.Na}} \times 100$
27. S.A.R. is an equal to
    (a) $\frac{\text{Na}}{\sqrt{\frac{\text{Ca}+\text{Mg}}{2}}}$ (b) $\sqrt{\frac{\text{Ca}+\text{Mg}}{2}}$
    (c) Both (c) None of the above
28. Soil erosion caused by rainfall is the result of the application of energy from twç distinct sources namely
    (a) The surface flow (b) The falling rain drops
    (c) Both of the above (d) None of the above

29. When sheet erosion is allowed to continue unchecked, the silt laden run off forms well- defined, but minute finger shaped growers over, the entire field? Such this trammeling is known as
(a) Stream bank erosion (b) Gully erosion
(c) Rill erosion (d) None of these
30. Geologic erosion is
(a) Takes place normally in arid and semiarid areas devoid of vegetation where the wide velocity is high
(b) Is caused by water
(c) Takes place normally in arid that ages are required for it to make any marked alteration in the major features
(d) The removal of surface soil from areas devoid of their natural protective cover as a result of living being take place at a much faster rate
31. Hilly soils are low in lime and
(a) Alkaline (b) Salts
(c) Acidic (d) None of these
32. The area of tarai soils in India is
(a) 5.7 m.ha (b) 3.7 m./ha
(c) 2.7 m./ha (d) 19.7 m./ha
33. Tarai soils are high in
(a) Iron (b) Organic matter
(c) Sodium (d) Calcium
34. The area of peaty soils in India is about
(a) 150 sq. km. (b) 250 sq. km
(c) 25 sq. km. (d) 275 sq. km.
35. Peat soils have ... organic matter
(a) 5-8% (b) 20-40%
(c) 50-55% (d) 60-65%
36. Peat soils are ...... in nature
(a) Alkaline (b) Acidic
(c) Neutral (d) Saline
37. The headquarters of Central Soil Salinity Research Institute is at
(a) Nagpur (b) Bangalore
(c) New Delhi (d) Karnal
38. 'Diara' lands are
(a) Areas created by sand storms
(b) Areas flooded by sea
(c) Areas on both sides of canal
(d) Areas located on either side of river which get flooded every year

39. Salt tolerant crop is
    (a) Cowpea (b) Sugarbeet
    (c) Pea (d) Muskmelon
40. Which one of the following pairs to correctly matched
    (a) Red soil-Calcareous (b) Black soil-Rich in kaolinite
    (c) Alkali soil pH-9 (d) Latente soil pH -8
41. Peat soils are generally
    (a) Black, heavy and acidic (b) Black, heavy and neutral
    (c) Red, light and acidic (d) Black, light and basic
42. Soil-amendment used to reclaim usar (barren) land is
    (a) Calcium sulphate (b) Sodium sulphate
    (c) Potassium sulphate (d) Calcium carbonate
43. Geological erosion is also known as
    (a) Soil erosion (b) Water erosion
    (c) Natural erosion (d) Accelerated erosion
44. The salt affected soils are' divided in how many classes depending upon electrical Conductivity and sodium contents of their solution extract
    (a) Tow (b) Three
    (c) Five (d) Four
45. Sugar content shall be highest if the refractometer reading is
    (a) 11-12 (b) 25
    (c) 17-18 (d) 20
46. Brix per cent in sugarcane juice is he indicator of –
    (a) Salt content in juice (b) Total solids in juice
    (c) Sucrose per cent in juice (d) None of these
47. The positive and high value of redox potential indicates
    (a) Strong oxidizing conditions
    (b) Equally reducing and oxidizing conditions
    (c) Reducing conditions
    (d) None of these
48. In a waterlogged soil the concentration of is high
    (a) Ethane (b) Carbon dioxide
    (c) Methane (d) Carbon monoxide
49. Plants grown in saline soils are known as
    (a) Bryophyte (b) Sciophyte
    (c) Xerophyte (d) Halophyte

50. South West Monsoon contributes about of total rainfall
    (a) 50% (b) 80%
    (c) 30% (d) 95%
51. Which of the following characteristic helps in the identification of alkali soil
    (a) Blackish spots or black colour on the surface
    (b) White or ash colour layer of salts on the surface
    (c) Reddish color on the surface
    (d) None of the above
52. Irrigation with sodic water increase the availability of:
    (a) Zinc (b) Sodium
    (c) Molybdenum (d) Chloride
53. The sodicty of water can be expressed by
    (a) ECe (b) ESP
    (c) SAR (d) None of these
54. Development of acidity iii soil which is encouraged by humid climate is delayed by presence of
    (a) Dolomite is soil (b) Iron in soil
    (c) earthworms in soil (d) Limestone in soil
55. Soil conservation measures are being undertaken in the catchments areas of river valley projects in order to
    (a) Check premature siltation of reservoirs catchments areas
    (b) Increase the rainfall in the catchments areas
    (c) Increase the area under forests
    (d) Provide employment to displaced persons
56. Tolerance to sol salinity of the given set of crops
    (a) Barley>Wheat>beans>uplands
    (b) Barley>wheat>upland
    (c) Paddy
    (d) Wheat>barley>beans>upland paddy
57. The characteristics of saline soil is:
    (a) ECe<4 mmhos/cm, pH<8.5 ESP>5
    (b) ECe>4 mmhos/cm., pH<8.5 ESP<15
    (c) ECe>4 mmhos/cm, pH<8.5 ESP<15
    (d) ECe>4 mmhos/cm, pH>8.5 ESP>15
58. Lime ($CaCO_3$) is added to reclaim
    (a) Alkali soil (b) Acid soil
    (c) Saline soil (d) Laterite soil

59. Poor quality waters contain
    (a) Higher amount of soluble salts
    (b) Higher amount of soluble calcium
    (c) Lower amount of soluble salts
    (d) None of the above
60. Alkali soil are reclaimed by the addition of
    (a) Gypsum (b) Lime
    (c) Calcium chloride (d) All of these
61. Terai soils are deficient in:
    (a) Zinc (b) Nitrogen
    (c) Sulphur (d) Phosphorus
62. The alkali soil has an excess of
    (a) Calcium (b) Sodium
    (c) Zinc (d) Potassium
63. The main characteristic which render the alkali soils unfavorable for crop growth is
    (a) Low pH
    (b) Poor physical condition
    (c) Excessive concentration of Soluble salts
    (d) All of these
64. Saline alkali soil are those soils which have
    (a) ECe>4 mmbos/cm. pH<8.5. ESP
    (b) ECe>4 mmhos/cm, pH >8.5, ESP>15
    (c) ECe>4 mmhos/cm, pH>8.5, ESP
    (d) ECe>4 mmhos/cm, pH 8.5, ESP<15
65. The salt tolerant crop is
    (a) Pea (b) Barley
    (c) Wheat (d) None of these
66. The factor responsible for the formation of acid soil is:
    (a) Low rainfall (b) High evaporation
    (c) High rainfall (d) Irrigation with saline water
67. The addition of gypsum reclaim the alkali soil and supply
    (a) Zinc (b) Calcium
    (c) Boron (d) Potassium
68. Alkali soil are generally found in
    (a) Sub-humid climate (b) Arid and semi-arid climate
    (c) Humid climate (d) Temperate climate

69. If a soil has more than 15% exchangeable sodium it is considered to be
(a) Neutral (b) Acidic
(c) Alkali (d) saline

70. Electrical conductivity of saluration extract of saline-sodic soils in dS/rn is
(a) 2.0 (b) 3.5
(c) 2.0-3.0 (d) More than 4.0

71. In saline-alkali soil the electrical conductivity is
(a) 2 dS/m (b) >4 dS/m
(c) 3 dS/m (d) None of these

72. According to Russian classification saline soils classified as
(a) Solonets (b) Solontex
(c) Solon chacks (d) None of these

73. The ESP of sodic alkaline soil is
(a) <15 (b) = 15
(c) >15 (d) >10

74. Name the first phase of water erosion
(a) Sheet erosion (b) Rill erosion
(c) Splash erosion (d) None of these

75. In saline soil major problem is due to
(a) High exchangeable sodium
(b) Low soil pH
(c) High pH
(d) High content of soluble salts

76. Which of the following adsorbed cations are largely responsible for soil acidity?
(a) Hydrogen (b) Sodium
(c) Calcium (d) Aluminum

77. Which of the following soils have electrical conductivity less than 4 dS/m?
(a) Acid (b) Saline
(c) Saline-sodic (d) Sodic

78. Which of the following are salt sensitive crops?
(a) Barley (b) Onion
(c) Potato (d) Sugarbeet

79. The chemical characteristics feature of non saline alkali soil,

	ECdS/m	ESP	pH		ECdS/m	ES	pH
(a)	<4	>15	>8.5	(b)	<4	>15	>8.5
(c)	<4	>15	>8.5	(d)	<4	>15	>8.5

80. Alkali soils are treated with gypsum to correct the deficiency of
    (a) Sulphur (b) Calcium
    (c) Zinc (d) Magnesium
81. Which micronutrient is most deficient in Indo-Gangatic alluvium soils?
    (a) Copper (b) Zinc
    (c) Iron (d) Manganese
82. Which fertilizer is most beneficial for alkali soils?
    (a) Urea (b) Ammonium nitrate
    (c) Ammonium sulphate (d) Calcium ammonium nitrate
83. The most productive normal soils have pH
    (a) 5-7 (b) 7-9
    (c) 4-6 (d) 6-8
84. Which is the most harmful salt in salt affected soils?
    (a) Sodium carbonate (b) Sodium sulphate
    (c) Sodium chloride (d) Sodium bicarbonate
85. Which element in not phytotoxic?
    (a) Selenium (b) Lethium
    (c) Flourine (d) Boron
86. What happens when an saline-alkali soil is leached with water?
    (a) pH and FC both decrease (b) pH increase and FC decrease
    (c) pH and FC both increase (d) pH and FC both decreased
87. Which fruit free is sensitive to acidity and salinity
    (a) Plum (b) Guava
    (c) Phalsa (d) Aonla
88. The waterlogged saline soils can be reclaimed through
    (a) Chemical amendment (b) Fertilizers
    (c) Biodrainage (d) Farmyard manure
89. Total dissolved solids in water having FC of 5dS/m will be about –
    (a) 3200 ppm (b) 4400 ppm
    (c) 4000 ppm (d) 3600 ppm
90. The Sodium Absorption Ratio (SAR) of the soil containing Na, Mg and Ca ions as 100, 30 and 20 meq/1, respectively, will be
    (a) 10 (b) 15
    (c) 20 (d) 5
91. The Residual Sodium Carbonate of water containing 35. 20,10 and meq/l. respectively will be
    (a) 0 meq/l (b) 5 meq/1
    (c) 10 meq/l. (d) 20 meq/1

92. According to modem concepts, the major function of inter row tillage is
(a) Moisture conservation through soil mulching
(b) Improved soil aeration
(c) Moisture conservation through
(d) Improved soil granulation weed destruction
93. Sodic soils generally exhibit soil structure of the type
(a) Platy (b) Granulated
(c) Subangular (d) Prismatic/columnar
94. Alkali soils can be reclaimed by the addition of
(a) Pyrites (b) Basic slag
(c) Lime (d) Calcite
95. The available water present in soil for better plant growth is between
(a) Field capacity and wilting percentage
(b) Field capacity and air dry soil
(c) Wilting percentage and Hydroscopic coefficient
(d) None of the above
96. Erosion caused by spattering of sol particles by the impact of rain drops is known as
(a) Sheet erosion (b) Gully erosion
(c) Rill erosion (d) Splash erosion
97. All potassium fertilizer's are physiologically alkaline, there reaction with soil is
(a) Acidic (b) Alkaline
(c) Neutral (d) None of these
98. Which of the following characteristic helps in the identification of alkali soil
(a) Blackish spots or black colour on the surface
(b) White or ash colour layer of salts on the surface
(c) Reddish color on the surface
(d) None of the above
99. Irrigation with sodic water increases the availability of
(a) Zinc (b) Sodium
(c) Molybdenum (d) Chloride
100. The sodicity of water can be expressed by
(a) ECe (b) ESP
(c) SAR (d) None of these

101. The characteristics of saline soil is:
   (a) ECe<4 mmhos/cm., pH< 8.5 ESP>15
   (b) EC3>4 mmhos/cm., pH<8.5, ESP<15
   (c) ECe<4 mmhos/cm., pH< 8.5, ESP<15
   (d) ECe>4 mmhos/cm., pH>8.5 ESP<15
102. Lime ($CaCO_3$) is added to reclaim
   (a) Alkali soil (b) Acid soil
   (c) Saline soil (d) Laterite soil
103. Poor quality waters contain
   (a) Higher amount of soluble salts
   (b) Higher amount of soluble calcium
   (c) Lower amount of soluble salts
   (d) None of the above
104. Alkali soil are reclaimed by the addition of
   (a) Gypsum (b) Lime
   (c) Calcium chloride (d) All of these
105. Saline soils occur mostly in
   (a) Punjab (b) Jammu and Kashmir
   (c) Madhya Pradesh (d) Haryana
106. The main characteristic which render the alkali soils unfavourable for crop growth is
   (a) Low pH
   (b) Poor physical condition
   (c) Excessive concentration of soluble salts
   (d) All of these
107. Saline alkali soil are those soils which have
   (a) ECe>4 mmhos/cm, pH<8.5, ESP >15
   (b) ECe>4 mmhos/cm, pH>8.5, ESP >15
   (c) ECe>4 mmhos/cm. pH>8.5 ESP > 15
   (d) ECe'c4 mmhos/cm, pH<8.5. ESP <15
108. The salt tolerant crop is
   (a) Pea (b) Barley
   (c) Wheat (d) None of these
109. The factor responsible for the formation of acid soil is:
   (a) Low rainfall (b) High evaporation
   (c) High rainfall (d) Irrigation with saline water

110. The addition of gypsum reclaim the alkali soil and supply
 (a) Zinc (b) Calcium
 (c) Boron (d) Potassium
111. Alkali soil are generally found m
 (a) Sub-humid climate (b) Arid and semi-arid climate
 (c) Humid climate (d) Temperate climate
112. Electrical conductivity of saturation extract of saline-sodic soils in dS/m is
 (a) 2.0 (b) 3.5
 (c) 2.0-3.0 (d) More than 4.0
113. Total dissolved solids in water having EC of 5 ds/m will be about
 (a) 3200 ppm (b) 4400 ppm
 (c) 4000 ppm (d) 3600 ppm
114. The sodium Absorption Ratio (SAR) of the soil containing Na, Mg and Ca ions as 100, 30 and 20 meq/1, respectively, will be
 (a) 10 (b) 15
 (c) 20 (d) 5
115. The Residual Sodium Carbonate of water containing 35, 20, 10 and meq/1, respectively, will be
 (a) 0 meq/1 (b) 5 meq/1
 (c) 10 meq/1 (d) 20 meq/1
116. According to modern concepts, the major function of inter row tillage is
 (a) Moisture conservation through soil mulching
 (b) Improved soil aeration
 (c) Moisture conservation through weed destruction
 (d) Improved soil granulation
117. Sodic soils generally exhibit soil structure of the type
 (a) Platy (b) Granulated
 (c) Subangular (d) Prismatic/columnar
118. Soil water content (%) at field capacity is maximum highest with
 (a) Loam (b) Slit Loam
 (c) Clayey soils (d) Clay loam
119. Carryover fertilizer effects are more pronounced in the case of
 (a) Urea (b) Calcium ammonium nitrate
 (c) Ammonium nitrate (d) Single super phosphate
120. Symbiotic nitrogen fixatio in canjanus cajan (tur/arhar) madiated by
 (a) Rhinzobium spp (cowpeamiscellany grouo)
 (b) Rhizobium phaseli
 (c) Rhixobium lupine
 (d) Rhizobium leguminosarum

121. The ionic form of phosphorus is determined by pH of the solution At pH 4.0 the predominated ionic forms of phosphorus, present are

(a) H_2PO_4 (b) $H_2PO_4^{-1}$ and PO_4^{-1}

(c) HPO_1 (d) $H_2PO_4^{-1}$ and HPO_4^{-1}

122. Journal of soil science s published from

(a) India (b) Canada

(c) Australia (d) USA

123. X-Ray different technique (s) is used to study

(a) Tracer studies (b) Photosynthesis

(c) Clay mineralogy (d) None of these

124. Alkali soils can be reclaimed by the addition of

(a) Pyrites (b) Basic slag

(c) Lime (d) Calcite

125. The available water present in soil for better plant growth is between

(a) Field capacity and wilting percentage

(b) Field capacity and air dry soil

(c) Wilting percentage and Hydroscopic coefficient

(d) None of these

126 At 1×10^{-9} H^+ concentration, what will be the pH value?

(a) 6 (b) 10

(c) 5 (d) 9

ANSWERS

1(b) 2(b) 3(d) 4(a) 5(b) 6(a) 7(c) 8(d) 9(b) 10(d) 11(a) 12(c) 13(d) 14(b) 15(d) 16(d) 17(d) 18(b) 19(c) 20(c) 21(b) 22(a) 23(d) 24(d) 25(d) 26(b) 27(a) 28(d) 29(d) 30(c) 31(b) 32(a) 33(b) 34(a) 35(b) 36(b) 37(d) 38(d) 39(b) 40(c) 41(a) 42(a) 43(c) 44(b) 45(c) 46(b) 47(a) 48(c) 49(d) 50(b) 51(a) 52(b) 53(c) 54(d) 55(a) 56(b) 57(b) 58(b) 59(a) 60(a) 61(a) 62(b) 63(b) 64(b) 65(b) 66(c) 67(b) 68(b) 69(c) 70(d) 71(b) 72(c) 73(c) 74(c) 75(d) 76(a) 77(a) 78(b) 79(a) 80(b) 81(b) 82(c) 83(d) 84(d) 85(d) 86(b) 87(a) 88(b) 89(a) 90(c) 91(c) 92(a) 93(d) 94(a) 95(a) 96(c) 97(d) 98(a) 99(b) 100(c) 101(b) 102(b) 103(a) 104(a) 105(d) 106(b) 107(a) 108(b) 109(c) 110(b) 111(b) 112(d) 113(a) 114(c) 115(c) 116(a) 117(d) 118(d) 119(c) 120(d) 121(a) 122(b) 123(c) 124(a) 125(a) 126(d)

CHAPTER - 8

Agriculture Statistics

1. In a situation when the soil fertility of field varies in two direction at right angles, the suitable design for a field experiment will be
   (a) Split plot design (b) CRD
   (c) RBD (d) LSD
2. The Student's t-test was proposed by
   (a) W S Gosset (b) Karl Pearson
   (c) D Moivre (d) R A Fisher
3. Father of Agriculture Statistics
   (a) C Spearman (b) Karl Pearson
   (c) D Moivre (d) R A Fisher
4. The value of correlation coefficient (r) varies between
   (a) -2 to +2 (b) less than +1
   (c) -1 to +1 (d) less than + 2
5. The term regression was first used by
   (a) Sir Francis Galton (b) Karl Pearson
   (c) D Moivre (d) S D Poisson
6. The advantage of local control
   (a) Reduce the error variance
   (b) Ensure the independence of observations
   (c) Both a and b
   (d) None of these
7. CRD is used when the experimental material is
   (a) Limited (b) Homogenous
   (c) Heterogenous (d) Both a and b
8. The design in which used only replication and randomization
   (a) RBD (b) Factorial RBD
   (c) CRD (d) LSD
9. Commonly design used in field experiment
   (a) CRD (b) RBD
   (c) LSD (d) Split plot design

10. To reduce the experimental error with heterogeneous material
    (a) More replication
    (b) Use of randomization
    (c) Use of local control technique
    (d) More replication and local control technique
11. Steps involved in testing hypothesis
    1. Null Hypothesis (H_0)
    2. Alternate hypothesis (H_1)
    3. Level of significance (5% or 1%)
    4. Test statistic
    5. Interpretation/conclusion
    (a) 1, 2, 3, 4, 5 (b) 5, 4, 3, 2, 1
    (c) 4, 3, 2, 5, 1 (d) 3, 2, 1, 4, 5
12. In the factorial experiment, effect exict
    (a) Simple effect (b) Main effect
    (c) Interaction effect (d) All of these
13. In the 2^3 Factorial experiment
    (a) 2 factors and 3 levels (b) 3 factors and 2 levels
    (c) 3 levels (d) None of these
14. ANOVA was developed by
    (a) W S Gosset (b) Karl Pearson
    (c) D Moivre (d) R A Fisher
15. Number of rows and columns are equal in
    (a) LSD (b) RBD
    (c) CRD (d) Strip plot design
16. Two errors will exist in this design
    (a) LSD (b) RBD
    (c) CRD (d) Split plot design
17. Single factor design of experiment
    (a) LSD (b) RBD
    (c) CRD (d) Strip plot design
18. Use two factors and both requires larger plots, these design is followed
    (a) Split-split plot design (b) Strip plot design
    (c) CRD (d) RBD
19. Use two factors and one factors requires larger plots and other factors requires more accuracy, these design is followed
    (a) Split-split plot design (b) Strip plot design
    (c) Split plot design (d) RBD

20. This design is more applicable to laboratory or pot culture experiments
    (a) Split-split plot design (b) Strip plot design
    (c) LSD (d) CRD
21. Rice crop give better performance in experiment these plot size
    (a) 20-40 m^2 (b) 80-100 m^2
    (c) 400 m^2 (d) 200 m^2
22. Sugarcane crop give better performance in experiment these plot size
    (a) 20-40 m^2 (b) 80-100 m^2
    (c) 400 m^2 (d) 200 m^2
23. In factorial experiments, Average of the simple effects of a factor is known as
    (a) Simple effect (b) Main effect
    (c) Chance effect (d) Interaction effect
24. In factorial experiments, the failure of simple effect of a given factor to remain consistent at various levels of the other factor is known as
    (a) Simple effect (b) Main effect
    (c) Chance effect (d) Interaction effect
25. In a 2^n factorial experiments, 2 represents
    (a) 2 levels (b) 2 factors
    (c) 2 interactions (d) None of these
26. In a 2^n factorial experiments, n represents
    (a) n levels (b) n factors
    (c) n interactions (d) None of these
27. The entire bulk of the observational material from which samples are drawn is referred to as
    (a) Sampling (b) Variable
    (c) Population (d) Frequency
28. Basic principle of design of experiments
    (a) Replication (b) Randomization
    (c) Local control (d) All of these
29. The repetition of the treatments under investigation is known as
    (a) Replication (b) Frequency
    (c) Variable (d) None of these
30. The method of giving equal chance to all individual treatments to show their performance is called
    (a) Randomization (b) Replication
    (c) Local control (d) Sampling

31. Critical difference (CD) value is sufficient for statistical accuracy in agricultural experiments
    (a) 0.01 (b) 0.05
    (c) 0.1 (d) 0.2
32. The systematic procedure for adjustment of the data with respect to co-variable is known as
    (a) Standard error (b) Analysis of variance
    (c) Analysis of co-variance (d) Standard error of difference
33. 'Test of significance' is also called as
    (a) Null hypothesis (b) Analysis of variance
    (c) Testing hypothesis (d) None of these
34. Testing the difference between two sample means is due to chance or real is called
    (a) Test of significance (b) Interpretation
    (c) Alternate hypothesis (d) None of these
35. In the CRD, the error degree of freedom
    (a) r (t-1) (b) (t-1)(r-1)
    (c) (rt-1) (d) None of these
36. In the CRD, the total degree of freedom
    (a) r (t-1) (b) (t-1)(r-1)
    (c) (rt-1) (d) (n-1)
37. In the CRD, the treatment degree of freedom
    (a) r (t-1) (b) (t-1)(r-1)
    (c) (rt-1) (d) (t-1)
38. In the RBD, the error degree of freedom
    (a) r (t-1) (b) (t-1)(r-1)
    (c) (rt-1) (d) None of these
39. In the RBD, the total degree of freedom
    (a) r (t-1) (b) (t-1)(r-1)
    (c) (rt-1) (d) None of these
40. In the LSD, the error degree of freedom
    (a) r (t-1) (b) (t-1)(t-2)
    (c) (rt-1) (d) None of these
41. In the LSD, the total degree of freedom
    (a) r (t-1) (b) (t-1)(r-1)
    (c) (t^2-1) (d) None of these
42. If the LSD have 5 treatment than error degree of freedom
    (a) 10 (b) 5
    (c) 24 (d) 12

ANSWERS

1(d) 2(a) 3(d) 4(c) 5(a) 6(a) 7(d) 8(c) 9(b) 10(d) 11(a) 12(d) 13(b) 14(d) 15(c) 16(d) 17(c) 18(b) 19(c) 20(d) 21(a) 22(b) 23(b) 24(d) 25(a) 26(b) 27(c) 28(d) 29(a) 30(a) 31(b) 32(c) 33(c) 34(a) 35(a) 36(d) 37(d) 38(b) 39(c) 40(b) 41(c) 42(d)

Model Question Paper - 1

1.1. Age of earth is approximately
(a) 1 million (b) 4.5 million
(c) 3 million (d) 12 million

1.2. The process used for removel of water hardness is
(a) Haber's process (b) Bray process
(c) Zeolite process (d) None of these

1.3. The main constituent of biogas is
(a) SO_2 (b) CO
(c) CH_4 (d) O_3

1.4. How many agro climate zone are found in India
(a) 9 (b) 14
(c) 15 (d) 21

1.5. Who coined the term symbiosis
(a) De Bary (b) Rutherford
(c) Liebieg (d) C.B. Lipman

1.6. Vehicular pollution emits mainly
(a) SO_2 (b) CO
(c) N_2 (d) O_3

1.7. Root development is stimulated due to supply of
(a) N (b) Ca
(c) P (d) K

1.8. What is the percentage of sulphur coated urea
(a) 18 (b) 38
(c) 24 (d) 34

1.9. Dicalcium phosphate is the product of the reaction of
(a) Rock phosphate + $H_4P_2O_7$ (b) Rock phosphate + H_3PO_4
(c) Rock phosphate + H_2SO_4 (d) Rock phosphate + HCl

1.10. Who discovered the essentiality of zinc to plants
(a) Broyer *et al.* (b) Priestly
(c) Rutherford (d) A.L.Somner and C.P.Lipman

1.11. Siderophores are related to which of the following metal elements
(a) Copper (b) Manganese
(c) Iron (d) Zinc

1.12. Strengite is the reaction product of phosphorus in
(a) Acid soil (b) Alkali soil
(c) Calcareous soil (d) Neutral soil

1.13. CS_2 is a potential inhibitor
(a) Immobilization (b) Urease activity
(c) Nitrification (d) None of these

1.14. Taking a representative sample represents a
(a) Wrong sampling (b) judgement sampling
(c) Representative sampling (d) Random sampling

1.15. Indicator plant used for the deficiency of potassium is
(a) Sugar beet (b) Potato
(c) Rapeseed (d) Oat

1.16. Which is known by brine solution?
(a) KNO_3 (b) $NaHCO_3$
(c) NaCl (d) CaO

1.17. Hyperpigmentation is caused due to
(a) As (b) Al
(c) Si (d) Bi

1.18. ________is an example of mineral that supply magnesium upon weathering
(a) Turmaline (b) Apatite
(c) Talc (d) Pyrite

1.19. ________ mineral is the most resistance to chemical weathering.
(a) Kaolinite (b) Quartz
(c) Calcite (d) Gypsum

1.20. There are ______ capability classes In the system of land capability classification
(a) Four (b) Five
(c) Eight (d) Ten

1.21. Organic mater in the soil ______ with rise in temperature.
(a) Increase (b) Affected positively
(c) Decrease (d) Unaffected

1.22. The water retained by air dried soils, is considered as _______ water
(a) Gravitatiotial (b) Capillary
(c) Hygroscopic (d) Available

1.23. The most cementing agent organic matter in soil can be removed by treatment of

(a) HC1 (b) H_2O_2

(c) C_2H_4 (d) H_2O

1.24. The size of silt partical as per International soil science society is

(a) 0.02 - 0.002mm (b) less than 0.002 mm

(c) 0.2 - 0.02mm d) 2.0 - 0.2mm

1.25. The soil moisture at bygroscopic co-efficient is ______ bar atmosphere

(a) 1.0 (b) 0.33

(c) 31.0 (d) 15.0

1.26. The amount of air in a soil is generally ______ related to the amount of water in soil

(a) Directly (b) Indirectly

(c) Not (d) Inversely

1.27. Sand, silt and clay particles differ principally in

(a) Mineral composition (b) Size

(c) Hardness (d) Density

1.28. The total surface area of 4 cm cube is

(a) 16 cm^2 (b) 24 cm^2

(c) 64 cm^2 (d) 96 cm^2

1.29. The soil can be rolled Into a wire at ______ moisture stage

(a) Lower plastic limit (b) Upper plastic limit

(c) Wilting point (d) Hygroscopic point

1.30. The most active portion of soil is

(a) Clay (b) Silt

(c) Cofloid (d) Sand

1.31. The most important properties of clay minerals are _____

(a) Expanding (b) Absorption

(c) Desorption (d) Contraction

1.32. The cation exchange capacity of vermiculite clay mineral is ______

(a) oxy – oxy (b) oxy – hydroxyl

(b) Hydroxy – hydroxy (d) Silica – alumina

1.33. The crystal units of kaolinate are held together by ________ linkages

(a) Oxy – oxy (b) Oxy – hydroxyl

(b) Hydroxy - hydroxy (d) Silica – alumina

1.34. Kaollnite is _______ type of clay mineral

(a) 1:1 (b) 2:l

(c) 2:2 (d) 2:l:1

1.35. Clay particles are mostly shaped like
(a) Sphere (b) Egg
(c) Flaks (d) Cube

1.36. Sesquioxides is a oxides of ________cations
(a) Divalent (b) Trivalent
(c) Tetravalent (d) None

1.37. _______Clay is dominant is vertisol
(a) Kaolinite (b) Illite
(c) Tetravalent (d) None

1.38. The exchangeable cations are generally _____ washed out of soil
(a) Easily (b) Equally
(c) Much less (d) Much more

1.39. Immobilization of nitrogen takes place at________C/N ratio
(a) 10:1 (b) 20:1
(c) 30:1 (d) 60:1

1.40. CEC values typical of montmorillonite is _______cmo1(+)/kg soil
(a) 10 (b) 28
(c) 40 (d) 80

1.41. The transformation of NH4 to NO3 is __________
(a) Aminization (b) Amoniflcation
(c) Denitrification (d) Nitrification

1.42. Under anaerobic conditions,__________bacteria can fixed atmospheric nitrogen in soil
(a) Azotobacter (b) Clostidium
(c) Rhizobium (d) Psudomonas

1.43. Most of the nitrogen in soil is in the form of______
(a) Organic matter (b) Soluble ions
(c) Exchangeable cation (d) Gases

1.44. Plants generally take up nitrogen from the soil in the form of
(a) Humus (b) Organic compound
(c) Nitrogen gas (d) Nitrate ion

1.45. ______ is the lowest moisture content at which the soil can be readily deformed or mold at without cracking.
(a) Plastic limit (b) Liquid limit
(c) Hygroscopic point (d) Saturation point

1.46. Phosphorus is taken up by plant in the form of
(a) Aluminum phosphate (b) Iron phosphate
(c) Calcium phosphate (d) H_2PO_{4-} ion

1.47. In flooded conditions, the best type of nitrogen fertilizer to applied is
(a) Urea (b) Sodium nitrate
(c) Ammonium chloride (d) Diaminonium phosphate

1.48. The most of phosphorus Is taken up by plant comes into contact with plant roots by means the process of
(a) Mass flow (b) Diffusion
(c) Root interception (d) Hydration

1.49. _______ is recognized the father of agricultural chemistry
(a) Scofleld (b) Liebig
(c) Arnon (d) Gris

1.50. ______ Is known as beneficial elements
(a) Cupper (b) Barium
(c) Nickel (d) Zinc

1.51. The critical limit of available phosphorus in soil is _____ kaha below which plant respond to its application.
(a) 10 (b) 28
(c) 50 (d) 140

1.52 Nematodes are known as__________
(a) Predators (b) Parasites
(c) Detritivers (d) Primary prod

1.53 Nematode have the shape of
(a) Tinymites (b) Round worms
(c) Branches filaments (d) Spirals

1.54. The most anaerobic organisms in the soil are
(a) Bacteria (b) Fungi
(c) Algae (d) Actinomycets

1.55. Mycorhizae most commonly are significant with regard to increasing plant uptake of____ nutrients
(a) Nitrogen (b) Phosphorus
(c) Potassium (d) Sulphur

1.56. When organic matter Is added to a soil, the availability of nitrogen may be quickly increased or decreased depending on the ____ of the added material.
(a) Acidity (b) Freshness
(c) C/N ratio (d) Moisture content

1.57. The well decomposed most of the organic matter has C/N ration of
(a) 60:1 (b) 40:1
(c) 20:1 (d) 10:1

1.58. When the C/N ratio reaches to an available nitrogen will begin to appear in the soil

(a) 60:1 (b) 40:1
(c) 20:1 (d) 10:1

1.59. Released by microorganism of an inorganic plant nutrient in available form organic matter is called ______

(a) Nitrillcation (b) Mineralization
(c) Humification (d) Denitrification

1.60. In composing different soil of various textures, one would expect that the organic matter content would be

(a) Smaller in sandy soil
(b) Greater in sandy soil
(c) Greater in fine textured soils
(d) Smaller in fine textured soils

1.61. Denitrification is carried out principles by

(a) Anaerobic heterotrophs (b) Aerobic heterotrophs
(c) Anaerobic autotrophs (d) Aerobic cutrotrophs

1.62. Chlorophyll pigment activates process ______ in plant

(a) Arninisation (b) Oxidation
(c) Reductions (d) Photo synthesis

1.63. ______ hormone can be used for weed control

(a) MH (b) GAa
(c) TBA (d) 2, 4D

1.64. ______ occurs in the leaves of tobacco

(a) Cocain (b) Nicotine
(c) Colchicine (d) Atropin

1.65. The Ions pass from cell to cell through the ______ protoplasmic connections

(a) Mitochondria (b) Vacuole
(c) Plasmodesmeta (d) Nucleae

1.66. ______ maintains water rclations and turger pressure in plants.

(a) Calcium (b) Magnesium
(c) Potassium (d) Nitrogen

1.67. ______ nutrient is responsible for the Dieback of citrus.

(a) K (b) Mg
(c) Cu (d) Zn

1.68. ______ nutrient element is responsible for resistance to plant diseases

(a) Ca (b) Mg
(c) Na (d) K

1.69. Phosphorus might be considered a potential water pollutant because
(a) It is toxic to fish living in ill
(b) It is toxic to people who drink
(c) It fertilize algae and aquatic weed
(d) It acidifies natural waters

1.70. An excess application of common nitrogen as fertilizer to a farm fields, which modes of pollution would be likely occur
(a) Ground water by NH_4 (b) Ground water by NO_3
(c) Ground water by NO_2 (d) Ground water by N_2

1.71. The RSC of water is ______ for the Irrigation water contains 6, 4, 4 and 8 meq/1 of Ca^2, Mg^{2+}, CO_3^{2-} and HCO_{3-},respectively
(a) 1.0 (b) 2.0
(c) 0 (Zero) (d) (-2.0) negative

1.72. The water having Ca-10 meq/l, Mg-Smeq/l and Na 45 meq/l, Its SAR will be______
(a) 15.0 (b) 22.5
(c) 34.0 (d) 45.0

1.73. At O pH the solution contains W ion concentration of ______.
(a) 1 ppm (b) 1 mg/1
(c) 1 g/l (d) 1 percentage

1.74. The ion concentration in the solution is ______ times more at pH 5.0 as compare to that of at pH 8.0
(a) 30 (b) 1000
(c) 300 (d) 3000

1.75. The concept of pH is suggested by the scientist ________
(a) Lamben (b) Hiigard
(c) Sorenson (d) Beer

1.76. EC value in dS/m is equal to ________.
(a) Micromhos/cm (b) Miilimhos/cm
(c) Mhos/cm (d) Desimhos/m

1.77. To replace 6 cmol/kg each. Na it required ____ ton gypsum/ha.
(a) 1.20 (b) 2.00
(c) 2.40 (d) 5.16

1.78. Saline soils are dominant in _______ salt.
(a) NaHCO3 (b) Na2CO3
(c) NaC1 (d) CaSO4

1.79. Sodic soils are dominant in ________ salt
(a) $NaHCO_3$ (b) NaC1
(c) Na_2SO_4 (d) CsO_4

1.80. Saline alkali soil can be prevents to degradation during leaching with_______.

(a) Rain water (b) Sweet water
(c) Saline water (d) Distilled water

1.81. Soils become hazards when Ca/Mg ration is

(a) 0.1 (b) 0.0
(c) 1.0 (d) 2.0

1.82. The leaching requirement of saline water having conductivity of 3 dS/m is ______ per cent to tolerate field crop at 4 dS/m ECe.

(a) 30% (b) 40%
(c) 60% (d) 75%

1.83. The EC of sea water is _____dS/m.

(a) 48.5 (b) 46.0
(c) 24.0 (d) 58.0

1.84. Gypsum a soil amendment Is very well useful to reclaim _____

(a) Saline (b) Acid saline
(c) Alkali soil (d) Saline alkali

1.85. One Ion of calcium will replace ______ ion of sodium.

(a) One (b) Two
(c) Three (d) Four

1.86. Hasard due to high Na content in irrigation water is expressed by

(a) pH (b) EC
(c) SAR (d) ESP

1.87. The ESP of soil is _____ when the soil having CEC and exch. Na of 20 and 8 cmol/kg, respectively

(a) 10 (b) 20
(c) 40 (d) 48

1.88. The SAR of water is _______ containing Ca, Mg and Na were 20, 12 and 40 meq/l.

(a) 8 (b) 10
(c) 12 (d) 16

1.89. The salt content in soil at PWP will be ________ than that at the saturation point

(a) Two times higher (b) Four times higher
(c) One & half times higher (d) One fourth times higher

1.90. The soil having ECe 5 dS/m will create the ospatic pressure _____ in soil solution

(a) 1.2 (b) 1.5
(c) 1.6 (d) 1.8

1.91. The yield of many crop is restricted at soil ECe ______ dS/m.
(a) 2-4 (b) 4-8
(c) 8-16 (d) more than 16

1.92. ________ has suggested RSC concept to evaluate irrigation water
(a) Rechard (b) Eaton
(c) Scofield (d) Hilgard

1.93. Sodic soils fall in ___________ suborder, as per soil taxonomy classification
(a) Salorthid (b) Orthid
(c) Argid (d) Arid

1.94. In India about ______ million hectare lands is salt affected.
(a) 7.0 (b) 8.0
(c) 10.0 (d) 12.0

1.95. The reserved acidity of soil is measure by
(a) pH (b) Gypsum requirement
(c) Lime requirement (d) EC

1.96. ______ soil have seldom more than 8.5 pH
(a) Saline alkali (b) Non saline alkali
(c) Black alkali (d) Degraded alkali

1.97. Generally, non-saline alkali soils are developed in ______ climate
(a) Arid (b) Semi arid
(c) Sub humid (d) Humid

1.98. The soil amendment ______ is the acid former type.
(a) Lime (b) Gypsum
(c) Sulphur (d) Dolomite

1.99. ______ ion on exchange complex is responsible for reserve acidity in soil
(a) Aluminum (b) Calcium
(c) Potassium (d) Magnesium

1.100. The electrical conductivity of saturated gypsum solution is ______dS/m.
(a) 1.00 (b) 1.41
(c) 2.20 (d) 2.67

1.101. The titration with EDTA is known as ______ method
(a) Scoonover (b) Sorenson
(c) Versenate (d) Boyer

1.102. The pH of NH_4OH + NH_4C1 buffer solution is
(a) 8.2 (b) 9.2
(c) 9.5 (d) 10.0

1.103. The estimation of gypsum requirement of sodic soil is done by_____ method

(a) Versenate (b) Scoonover

(c) Bover (d) Stainberg

1.104. ppm is equivalent to _________

(a) meq/1 (b) me/100 g

(c) mg/ml (d) mg/1

1.105. During estimation of organic carbon in soil, it will be oxidized with_______ reagent

(a) K_2CrO_4 (b) K_2CO_3

(c) $K_2Cr_2O_7$ (d) $KHCO_3$

1.106. __________reagent is used to extract available phosphorus in soil

(a) $NaSO_4$ (b) NaC1

(c) Na_2CO_3 (d) $NaHCO_3$

1.107. During phosphorus determination, a blue colour is developed with_____ reagent

(a) $BaCl_2$ (b) K_2CrO_4

(c) NaC1 (d) $SnC1_2$

1.108. Copper wires carry electric current faster than _________ wire

(a) Aluminum (b) Silver

(c) Gold (d) Platinum

1.109. A° (angstron) is equal to_________

(a) 10^{-8} cm (b) 10^{-8} mm

(c) 10^{-10} cm (d) 10^{-9} mm

1.110. Iodides are act as _____ agent.

(a) Oxidizing agent (b) Reducing

(c) Strong oxidizing (d) Weak oxidizing

1.111. ______ is used as desiccating agent

(a) $CaCO_3$ (b) $CaSO_4$

(c) $CaC1_2$ (d) $CaHCO_3$

1.112. The intensity of blue colour is measured using ______ filter in photoelectric colourimeter.

(a) Red coloured (b) Yellow coloured

(c) Green coloured (d) Blue colored

1.113. _________ in aqueous solution gives acidic reaction

(a) $Na2SO_4$ (b) NaCl

(c) $CaC1_2$ (d) $CaCO_3$

1.114. The pH range of colour change for phenolphthalein indicator is

(a) 7.00-7.8 (b) 7.8-8.2

(c) 8.3-10.0 (d) 9.0-10.6

1.115. ________ is used as primary standard in most of the chemical laboratories.

(a) Potassium hydroxide (b) Potassium hydrogen phthalate

(c) Potassium permanganate (d) Potassium chromate

1.116. ______ is used in Ion chromatography.

(a) Resine (b) Silica gel

(c) Plaster of paris (d) Kaoline

1.117. The flamephotometric is used for the determination of ______ ions.

(a) Nitrogen (b) Phosphorus

(c) Potassium (d) Sulphur

1.118. ______ Method is used widely in the soil testing laboratory for evaluation available P status.

(a) Subbiah and Bajaj (b) Ramamoorthy

(c) Olsen (d) Bray

1.119. ______ method has become the most widely accepted procedure for measuring the exchangeable K.

(a) 1N ammonium acetate (b) Alkaline permanganate

(c) Versenate (d) Morgan

1.120. The Soil critical value of nutrient below, which plant responds to nutrient, is fixed by the method described by________.

(a) Cate and Nelson (b) Waugh and Fitts

(c) Schmehl and Humbert (d) Krishnamoorthy

1.121. Nitrate can also be toxic to mammals if present in ground water at: concentration more than ________ ppm.

(a) 1,0 (b) 15

(c) 30 (d) 45

1.122. According to Bureau of Indian Standard (BIS), the permissible limit BOD In the Industrial effluent is ____ ppm.

(a) 20 (b) 30

(c) 100 (d) 250

ANSWERS

1.1(b) 1.2(c) 1.3(c) 1.4(c) 1.5(a) 1.6(b) 1.7(c) 1.8(b) 1.9(d) 1.10(d) 1.11(c) 1.12(a) 1.13(c) 1.14(b) 1.15(b) 1.16(c) 1.17(a) 1.18(c) 1.19(a) 1.20(c) 1.21(c) 1.22(c) 1.23(b) 1.24(a) 1.25(c) 1.26(d) 1.27(c) 1.28(d) 1.19(a) 1.30(c) 1.31(d) 1.32(d) 1.33(b) 1.34(a) 1.35(c) 1.36(c) 1.37(c) 1.38(c) 1.39(d) 1.40(d) 1.41(d) 1.42(a) 1.43(a) 1.44(d) 1.45(a) 1.46(d) 1.47(c) 1.48(b) 1.49(b) 1.50(c) 1.51(b) 1.52(d) 1.53(b) 1.54(a) 1.55(b) 1.56(c) 1.57(d) 1.58(d) 1.59(b) 1.60(c) 1.61(b) 1.62(d) 1.63(d) 1.64(b) 1.65(c) 1.66(c) 1.67(c) 1.68(d) 1.69(c) 1.70(a) 1.71(b) 1.72(a) 1.73(c) 1.74(b) 1.75(c) 1.76(b) 1.77(d) 1.78(c) 1.79(a) 1.80(c) 1.81(a) 1.82(d) 1.83(d) 1.84(c) 1.85(b) 1.86(c) 1.87(c) 1.88(b) 1.89(b) 1.90(a) 1.91(b) 1.92(b) 1.93(c) 1.94(a) 1.95(c) 1.96(a) 1.97(c) 1.98(c) 1.99(a) 1.100(c) 1.101(c) 1.102(d) 1.103(b) 1.104(c) 1.105(c) 1.106(d) 1.107(d) 1.108(a) 1.109(a) 1.110(b) 1.111(c) 1.112(b) 1.113(c) 1.114(c) 1.115(b) 1.116(a) 1.117(c) 1.118(c) 1.119(a) 1.120(a) 1.121(b) 1.122(b)

Model Question Paper - 2

2.1. Which of the following rock has an acidic nature

(a) Gabro (b) Basaltic trap

(c) Diorite (d) Granite

2.2. Which of the following minerals is softer than fingernail?

(a) Quartz (b) Gypsum

(c) Calcite (d) Corundum

2.3. Which of the following mineral has the chemical composition $Fe_2O3 . 3H_2O$.

(a) Lixnonite (b) Haematite

(c) Mangesite (d) Magnesite

2.4. Micashist is one of the following types of metamorphic rock?

(a) Hydro metamorphic (b) Dynemo metamorphic

(c) Thermo metamorphic (d) Conglomarate type rock

2.5. Which of the following mineral contains potassium element.

(a) Gibsite (b) Calcite

(c) Biotite mica (d) Falsite

2.6. How much oxygen present in the earth crust.

(a) 25% (b) 32%

(c) 46% (d) 52%

2.7. Which of the following soil is formal recently

(a) Vertisol (b) Alfisol

(c) Histisol (d) Entisol

2.8. Which of the following is a secondary mineral.

(a) Feldspare (b) Biotite

(c) Kaolinite (d) Hornblend

2.9. Which of the following soils has pH more than 9.0.

(a) Saline (b) Saline alkali

(c) Non saline alkali (d) White alkali

2.10. Which of the following is least resistant to weathering mineral

(a) Gypsum (b) Kaolinite

(c) Musco white mica (d) Quartz

2.11. Which of the following mineral is element form
(a) Graphite (b) Apatite
(c) Tanc (d) Calcite

2.12. From which of the following slate is reformed metamorphically
(a) Sand stone (b) Shale
(c) Lime stone (d) Silicate clay

2.13. Which of the following is oldest of rock?
(a) Basaltic trap (b) Granite
(c) Sand stone (d) Lime stone

2.14. Soils derived from trap are generally
(a) Poor in fertility (b) Fertile
(c) Acidic in nature (d) Sandy in texture

2.15. Which of the following type soil is generally easiest to manage for crops.
(a) Loamy sand (b) Clay loam
(c) Silty loam (d) Sandy loam

2.16. Which of the following has prismatic structure with round shape?
(a) Collumnar (b) Laminar
(c) Angular blocky (d) Sub angular blocky

2.17. The extent of damage due to a crop by a period of waterlogged condition will damage on the following.
(a) Plant species (b) Stage of growth
(c) Organic nature (d) None of them

2.18. Which of the following is most sticky and plastic when wet.
(a) Vermiculite (b) Kaolinite
(c) Illite (d) Smectite

2.19. Which of the following has very low net negative charge of approximately 2.3 cmol/kg?
(a) Allophane (b) Vermiculite
(c) Smectite (d) Illite

2.20. One of the following is an example of non-expanding silicate day.
(a) Kaolinite (b) Fine grind mica (Illite)
(c) Smactite (d) Motmorillonite

2.21. Which of the following mineral is called ferromagneslum.
(a) Limonite (b) Muscovite
(c) Feldspare (d) Olivine

2.22. Which of the following is non silicate mineral.
(a) Apatite (b) Mica
(c) Badeline (d) Chlorite

2.23. Which of the following mineral is common In sulphur containing mineral

(a) Dolomite (b) Apatite

(c) Pyrite (d) Calcited

2.24. Clay particles are mostly shaped

(a) Prism (b) Egg

(c) Cube (d) Flakes

2.25. The distance between adjacent crystal layer is narrowest in.

(a) Illite (b) Kaolinite

(c) Vermiculite (d) Smectite

2.26. Give the name of one of the weathering process from the following match with the equation 4 FeO +02 4 2 Fe2O3.

(a) Carbonation (b) Oxidation

(c) Hydrolysis (d) Hydration

2.27. The process of washing out is term

(a) Illuviation (b) Eluvial

(c) Eluviations (d) Illuvial

2.28. Which of the following is generally taken up by plant In the greatest amount

(a) N (b) P

(c) K (d) Ca

2.29. Which of the following is less essential for plant growth than next to N

(a) P (b) K

(c) S (d) Z

2.30. Which of the following is most closely associate with physiological functions of protein synthesis?

(a) Ca (b) Zn

(c) K (d) N

2.31. Which of the following type structure tends to impede drainage

(a) Blocky (b) Prismatic

(c) Platy (d) Columnar

2.32. The mechanical separations of soil particles are based on one of the following law

(a) Boyle's (b) Darcy's

(c) Charl's (d) Stokesd

2.33. Term loam refers to soil
(a) With equal percentage of sand, silt and day
(b) Equally influenced by sand, silt and clay
(c) With well developed granular structure
(d) In good tilth

2.34. Which of the factors listed below would tend to promote warmer soil temperature in spring
(a) Organic mulch (b) Sandy texture
(c) High moisture content (d) Sowing at N-W direction

2.35. Which of the following texture is more susceptible to water caused erosion
(a) Sandy (b) Silty
(c) Loamy (d) Clayey

2.36. Which one of the following soil bas highest bulk density
(a) Sandy loam (b) Sandy
(c) Loamy sand (d) Sandy clay loam

2.37. Which of the following water is utilized by plant from the soil
(a) Gravitational water (b) Capillary water
(c) Non capillary water (d) Hygroscopic water

2.38. Higher the valency of ion bas replacing power
(a) Lower (b) Medium
(c) Greater (d) Nothing

2.39. Colloidal partical are generally less than
(a) 1 micrometer (b) 2 micrometer
(c) 10 micrometer (d) 100 micrometer

2.40. If the following values are for soil moisture potential, which soil is the driest?
(a) 5 bar (b) 3 atms
(c) 500 cm H2O (d) 1 Mpa

2.41. Pascal is a unit of
(a) Force (b) Energy
(c) Pressure (d) Area

2.42. Which ODR indicate the better soil aeration
(a) 15×10^{-8} g cm^{-1} min^{-1} (b) 30×10^{-8} g cm^{-1} min^{-1}
(c) 60×10^{-8} g cm^{-1} min^{-1} (d) 45×10^{-8} g cm^{-1} min^{-1}

2.43. Which of the listed below specific heats is typical of a dry soil?
(a) 0.1 cal g^{-1} 0C^{-1} (b) 0.2 cal g^{-1} °C-1
(c) 1.0 cal g^{-1} 0C^{-1} (d) 2.0 cal g^{-1} °C-1

2.44. Which group of organisms is generally the most numerous in soil?

(a) Fungi (b) Algae

(c) Bacteria (d) Earthworms

2.45. The following organism is generally dominant in fresh plant residues.

(a) Fungi (b) Bacteria

(c) Algae (d) Actinomycetes

2.46. Which of the following organism Is generally credited with producing : the sweet aroma of freshly plowed soil?

(a) Fungi (b) Bacteria

(c) Algae (d) Actinomycetes

2.47. The rapid decomposition of organic matter supporting a large number of beterotrophs in soil.

(a) Destroys the soil granular structure

(b) Release extra oxygen in soil

(c) Suppresses the incidence at root disease

(d) Uses up soil moisture before plant can get it

2.48. The 'ash' is a small but important fraction of the organic matter because it contains.

(a) Carbon (b) Carbon dioxide

(c) Mineral elements (d) Nitrogen

2.49. In what form is carbon commonly lost from a soil in the drainage water.

(a) CO_2 (b) C_2H_4

(c) HCO_3 (d) CO

2.50. A hetrotrophs bacteria has which one of the following characteristics.

(a) Can live at a wide range of pH

(b) Can photosynthesis in light

(c) Get it carbon from CO_2

(d) Needs energy rich organic substances for food

2.51. Under which of the following conditions would it be most important to mix soybean seed with rhizobia inoculum at sowing

(a) The field had been cropped to soybean in a monoculture

(b) The field had been cropped to corn-soybean rotation, with less fertilisation

(c) No soybean bad been grown in the field previously

(d) The field had been limed recently

2.52. Which of the following compound is not ionized or not an electrolyte substance
(a) Muriate of potash (b) Dianmonium phosphate
(c) Ammonium sulphate (d) Urea

2.53. Origin of negative charge in kaolinite is due to
(a) Isomorphus replacement (b) Dissociation of OH- ion
(c) PH dependent (d) Broken edge

2.54. The transformation of NH_4^+ to NO_{3-} is due to
(a) Aminization (b) Amoriiflcation
(c) Denitrification (d) Nitrification

2.55. Available phosphorus in soil is governed by
(a) C/N ratio (b) Sesquioxide/silica ratio
(c) Ca/Mgratio (d) Na/Kratio

2.56. Which of the following type of clay can most readily fix Nile ion?
(a) Chlorite (b) Kaolinite
(c) Vermiculite (d) All phase

2.57. Farmers often speak of 'light' or 'heavy' soils. These terms reflect to
(a) Particle density (b) Bulk density
(c) Soil texture (d) Soil porosity

2.58. What is the Q of a soil with bulk density D6 = 1.4 Mg/m3:and water content w = 45 % ?
(a) 14% (b) 45%
(c) 63% (d) 72%

2.59. Which of the following soil contains the greatest volume of water at 15 bar pressure?
(a) Sandy loam (b) Clayey
(c) Silty loam (d) Clay loam

2.60. At what pH range P generally most available for plant
(a) 5.5-6.5 (b) 6.5-7.5
(c) 7.5-8.5 (d) 8.5-9.5

2.61. Which of the following element is most commonly involved with "Luxury consumption"?
(a) Sulphur (b) Potassium
(c) Phosphorus (d) Nitrogen

2.62. Luxury consumption is detrimental because
(a) It is wasteful (b) It is cause K toxicity
(c) It cause low yield (d) More uptake by plant

2.63. The proportion of the total soil K that is available form is usually.

(a) About 50% (b) About 25%

(c) Very large proportion (d) Very small proportion

2.64. Plant root generally take up sulphur in the form of

(a) 50_4^{2-} (b) H_2S

(c) 5^{2-} (d) SO_2

2.65. Which of the following micronutrient elemcnt is found in plant in the greatest quantity?

(a) Zn (b) Fe

(c) Cu (d) Mo

2.66. Which of the following condition would be most increase the, availability of Fe?

(a) Well aerated dry soil with low pH

(b) Well aerated dry soil with high pH

(c) Wetsoil with low pH

(d) Wet soil with high pH

2.67. Which of the following constituent of chlorophyll and is located at Its center?

(a) Ca (b) Mg

(c) K (d) Na

2.68. The translocation of sugars in plant is governed by

(a) Mo (b) S

(c) N (d) B

2.69. Which of the following element is require for fixation of atmospheric nitrogen in soil?

(a) B (b) Mo

(c) S (d) P

2.70. Which of the following yellowing symptoms of plant is observed for nitrogen deficiency?

(a) Upper leaves (b) Middle leaves

(c) Lower leaves (d) Small spots on leaves

2.71. Which of the following nutrient is responsible for the gummosis in citrus?

(a) Cu (b) Zn

(c) B (d) Mo

2.72. An abnormal mitosis in plant takes place due to

(a) Ca deficiency (b) P deficiency

(c) B deficiency (d) Mn deficiency

2.73. Which of the following is responsible for the little leaf of cotton?
(a) Cu (b) Fe
(c) Zn (d) P

2.74. A hollow stem of cauliflower is caused by
(a) Mo (b) B
(c) Cu (d) Zn

2.75. Which of the following element is responsible for energy transfer process in plant?
(a) Sulphur (b) Phosphorus
(c) Boron (d) Iron

2.76. The reduction of NO_3 to NO_2 is due to
(a) B (b) Co
(c) Mo (d) S

2.77. Which of the following nutrient encourage vegetative growth?
(a) Mg (b) N
(c) S (d) K

2.78. Root growth is particularly affected by
(a) Copper (b) Phosphorus
(c) Zinc (d) Magnesium

2.79. Almost 95% of Indian soils are low or medium in
(a) Zinc (b) Phosphorus
(c) Potassium (d) Sulphur

2.80. A straight fertilizer is one which
(a) Comes straight from the factory
(b) Dissolves quickly
(c) Has orle major nutrient
(d) In liquid form

2.81. Which of the following fertilizer create the acidity in soil with continuous application?
(a) DAP (b) MOP
(c) SSP (d) Nitrate

2.82. The optimum fertilizer dose is one which maximizes
(a) Soil fertility (b) Yield
(c) Profits (d) Water use

2.83. The most important source of sulphur for the Indian soils is
(a) Gypsum (b) SSP
(c) Pyrite (d) AS

2.84. The state using most fertilizer per hectare,
(a) Tamilnadu (b) Punjab
(c) West Bengal (d) Kerala

2.85. The central fertilizer quality control Institute is located at
(a) Hyderabad (b) Krishi Bhavan
(c) Faridabad (4) Pune

2.86. Cereal straw is particularly rich source of
(a) Calcium (b) Potassium
(c) Ferrous iron (d) Zinc

2.87. Indian depends completely on import for its need of
(a) Rock phosphorus (b) Potash
(c) Gas (d) Zinc ash

2.88. Most commonly soil type found in India is
(a) Black (b) Red
(c) Alluvial (d) Late rite

2.89. A soil having pH 8.8 is called
(a) Normal (b) Alkaline
(c) Alkali (d) White alkali

2.90. Which of the following method of irrigation the salt the maximum at surface?
(a) Flood irrigation (b) Sprinkler irrigation
(c) Drip Irrigation (d) Ridge and furrow irrigation

2.91. The Na hazard in irrigation water can best be expressed by
(a) pH (b) SAR
(c) EC (c) ESP

2.92. The soil having pH 7.8, ECe 2.4 and ESP 24 is classified as
(a) Saline alkali (b) Non saline alkali
(c) White alkali (d) Normal one

2.93. What will be SAR of water containing Ca+2, Mg+2 and Ne tons 20, 12 and 40 mg/I, respectively?
(a) 4.0 (b) 5.0
(c) 10.0 (d) 20.0

2.94. Which of the following state rank first in per cent of salt affected soil that of net cultivated area of the state?
(a) UP (b) Haryana
(c) Gujarat (d) Rajasthan

2.95. Phosphorus might be considered a potential waters pollutant because
(a) It is toxic to fish living in water
(b) It is toxic to reapply who drink
(c) It fertilize algae and aquatic weed
(d) It acidily natural waters

2.96. Which of the gases listed below is most severally toxic to plant growth?
(a) CO_{2-} (b) N_2
(c) C_2H_4 (d) Argon

2.97. Which form of nitrogen is comparatively more toxic?
(a) NO_{2-} (b) NO_{3-}
(c) NH_{4+} (d) $CO(NH_2)_2$

2.98. According to National Academy of Science, the toxic limit of fluride in water is
(a) 1.0 mg/1 (b) 2.0 mg/1
(c) 3.0 mg/1 (d) 5.0 mg/1

2.99. Which of the following salts comparatively more toxic for the plant growth
(a) $MgSO_4$ (b) Na_2SO_4
(c) Na_2CO_3 (d) $CaSO_4$

2.100. Following one is the lower toxic limit of boron content in irrigation water
(a) 0.33 ppm (b) 0.67 ppm
(c) 0.1 ppm (d) 1.0 ppm

2.101. Most energy required to detach the particle size
(a) 0.1 mm diameter (b) 0.01 diameter
(c) 0.00 1 diameter (d) 0.0001 diameter

2.102. Which of the following type of particle is most susceptible to wind erosion?
(a) Coarse sand (b) Fine sand
(c) Silt (d) Clay

ANSWERS

2.1(d) 2.2(b) 2.3(a) 2.4(b) 2.5(c) 2.6(c) 2.7(d) 2.8(c) 2.9(c) 2.10(a) 2.11(a) 2.12(d) 2.13(b) 2.14(b) 2.15(c) 2.16(a) 2.17(d) 2.18(d) 2.19(d) 2.20(b) 2.21(d) 2.22(a) 2.23(c) 2.24(d) 2.25(b) 2.26(b) 2.27(c) 2.28(a) 2.29(a) 2.30(d) 2.31(c) 2.32(d) 2.33(b) 2.34(b) 2.35(b) 2.36(b) 2.37(b) 2.38(c)

2.39(a) 2.40(d) 2.41(c) 2.42(c) 2.43(b) 2.44(c) 2.45(a) 2.46(d) 2.47(c) 2.48(c) 2.49(c) 2.50(d) 2.51(c) 2.52(d) 2.53(c) 2.54(d) 2.55(b) 2.56(c) 2.57(c) 2.58(c) 2.59(b) 2.60(d) 2.61(b) 2.62(a) 2.63(d) 2.64(a) 2.65(b) 2.66(c) 2.67(b) 2.68(d) 2.69(b) 2.70(c) 2.71(a) 2.72(a) 2.73(c) 2.74(b) 2.75(b) 2.76(c) 2.77(b) 2.78(b) 2.79(b) 2.80(c) 2.81(a) 2.82(c) 2.83(c) 2.84(b) 2.85(c) 2.86(b) 2.87(b) 2.88(c) 2.89(c) 2.90(d) 2.91(b) 2.92(b) 2.93(c) 2.94(c) 2.95(c) 2.96(c) 2.97(a) 2.98(b) 2.99(a) 2.100(a) 2.101(d) 2.102(b)

ICAR Institutions, Deemed Universities National Research Centres, National Bureaux & Directorate/Project Directorates

Deemed Universities - 4

1. Indian Agricultural Research Institute, New Delhi
2. National Dairy Research Institute, Karnal
3. Indian Veterinary Research Institute, Izatnagar
4. Central Institute on Fisheries Education, Mumbai

Institutions - 45

1. Central Agricultural Research Institute, Port Blair
2. Central Arid Zone Research Institute, Jodhpur
3. Central Avian Research Institute, Izatnagar
4. Central Inland Fisheries Research Institute, Barrackpore
5. Central Institute Brackishwater Aquaculture, Chennai
6. Central Institute for Research on Buffaloes, Hissar
7. Central Institute for Research on Goats, Makhdoom
8. Central Institute of Agricultural Engineering, Bhopal
9. Central Institute of Arid Horticulture, Bikaner
10. Central Institute of Cotton Research, Nagpur
11. Central Institute of Fisheries Technology, Cochin
12. Central Institute of Freshwater Aquaculture, Bhubneshwar
13. Central Institute of Research on Cotton Technology, Mumbai
14. Central Institute of Sub Tropical Horticulture, Lucknow
15. Central Institute of Temperate Horticulture, Srinagar
16. Central Institute on Post harvest Engineering and Technology, Ludhiana
17. Central Marine Fisheries Research Institute, Kochi
18. Central Plantation Crops Research Institute, Kasargod
19. Central Potato Research Institute, Shimla
20. Central Research Institute for Jute and Allied Fibres, Barrackpore
21. Central Research Institute of Dryland Agriculture, Hyderabad
22. Central Rice Research Institute, Cuttack

23. Central Sheep and Wool Research Institute, Avikanagar, Rajasthan
24. Central Soil and Water Conservation Research & Training Institute, Dehradun
25. Central Soil Salinity Research Institute, Karnal
26. Central Tobacco Research Institute, Rajahmundry
27. Central Tuber Crops Research Institute, Trivandrum
28. ICAR Research Complex for Eastern Region including Centre of Makhana, Patna
29. ICAR Research Complex for NEH Region, Barapani
30. ICAR Research Complex Goa
31. Indian Agricultural Statistical Research Institute, New Delhi
32. Indian Grassland and Fodder Research Institute, Jhansi
33. Indian Institute of Horticultural Research, Bangalore
34. Indian Institute of Natural Resins and Gums, Ranchi
35. Indian Institute of Pulses Research, Kanpur
36. Indian Institute of Soil Sciences, Bhopal
37. Indian Institute of Spices Research, Calicut
38. Indian Institute of Sugarcane Research, Lucknow
39. Indian Institute of Vegetable Research, Varanasi
40. National Academy of Agricultural Research & Management, Hyderabad
41. National Institue of Abiotic Stress Management, Malegaon, Maharashtra
42. National Institute of Animal Nutrition and Physiology, Bengluru
43. National Institute of Research on Jute & Allied Fibre Technology, Kolkata
44. Sugarcane Breeding Institute, Coimbatore
45. Vivekananda Parvatiya Krishi Anusandhan Sansthan, Almora

National Research Centres - 17

1. National Centre for Agril. Economics & Policy Research, New Delhi
2. National Centre for Integrated Pest Management, New Delhi
3. National Research Centre for Agroforestry, Jhansi
4. National Research Centre for Banana, Trichi
5. National Research Centre for Citrus, Nagpur
6. National Research Centre for Grapes, Pune
7. National Research Centre for Litchi, Muzaffarpur
8. National Research Centre for Pomegranate, Solapur
9. National Research Centre on Camel, Bikaner

10. National Research Centre on Equines, Hisar
11. National Research Centre on Meat, Hyderabad
12. National Research Centre on Mithun, Medziphema, Nagaland
13. National Research Centre on Orchids, Pakyong, Sikkim
14. National Research Centre on Pig, Guwahati
15. National Research Centre on Plant Biotechnology, New Delhi
16. National Research Centre Seed Spices, Ajmer
17. National Research Centre on Yak, West Kemang

National Bureaux - 6

1. National Bureau of Plant Genetics Resources, New Delhi
2. National Bureau of Agriculturally Important Micro-organisms, Mau, Pradesh
3. National Bureau of Agriculturally Important Insects, Bangalore
4. National Bureau of Soil Survey and Land Use Planning, Nagpur
5. National Bureau of Animal Genetic Resources, Karnal
6. National Bureau of Fish Genetic Resources, Lucknow

Directorates/Project Directorates - 25

1. Directorate of Maize Research, New Delhi
2. Directorate of Rice Research, Hyderabad
3. Directorate of Wheat Research, Karnal
4. Directorate of Oilseed Research, Hyderabad
5. Directorate of Seed Research, Mau
6. Directorate of Sorghum Research, Hyderabad
7. Directorate of Groundnut Research, Junagarh
8. Directorate of Soybean Research, Indore
9. Directorate of Rapeseed & Mustard Research, Bharatpur
10. Directorate of Mushroom Research, Solan
11. Directorate on Onion and Garlic Research, Pune
12. Directorate of Cashew Research, Puttur
13. Directorate of Oil Palm Research, Pedavegi, West Godawari
14. Directorate of Medicinal and Aromatic Plants Research, Anand
15. Directorate of Floriculture Research, Pusa, New Delhi
16. Project Directorate for Farming Systems Research, Modipuram
17. Directorate of Water Management Research, Bhubaneshwar
18. Directorate of Weed Science Research, Jabalpur
19. Project Directorate on Cattle, Meerut
20. Project Directorate on Foot & Mouth Disease, Mukteshwar

21. Project Directorate on Poultry, Hyderabad
22. Project Directorate on Animal Disease Monitoring and Surveillance, Hebbal, Bangalore
23. Directorate of Knowledge Management in Agriculture (DKMA), New Delhi
24. Directorate of Cold Water Fisheries Research, Bhimtal, Nainital
25. Directorate of Research on Women in Agriculture, Bhubaneshwar

AICRPs & Network Projects

All India Coordinated Research Projects - 61

1. AICRP on Pesticides Residues, New Delhi
2. AICRP on Nematodes, New Delhi
3. AICRP on Maize, New Delhi
4. AICRP Rice, Hyderabad
5. AICRP on Chickpea, Kanpur
6. AICRP on MULLARP, Kanpur
7. AICRP on Pigeon Pea, Kanpur
8. AICRP on Arid Legumes, Jodhpur
9. AICRP on Wheat & Barley Improvement Project, Karnal
10. AICRP Sorghum, Hyderabad
11. AICRP on Pearl Millets, Jodhpur
12. AICRP on Small Millets, Bangalore
13. AICRP on Sugarcane, Lucknow
14. AICRP on Cotton, Coimbatore
15. AICRP on Groundnut, Junagarh
16. AICRP on Soybean, Indore
17. AICRP on Rapeseed & Mustard, Bharatpur
18. AICRP on Sunflower, Safflower, Castor, Hyderabad
19. AICRP on Linseed, Kanpur
20. AICRP on Sesame and Niger, Jabalpur
21. AICRP on Biological Control, Bangalore
22. AICRP on Honey Bee Research & Training, Hisar
23. AICRP -NSP(Crops), Mau
24. AICRP on Forage Crops, Jhansi
25. AICRP Tropical Fruits, Bangalore
26. AICRP Sub Tropical Fruits, Lucknow
27. AICRP Arid Zone Fruits, Bikaner
28. AICRP Mushroom, Solan

29. AICRP Vegetables including NSP vegetable, Varanasi
30. AICRP Potato, Shimla
31. AICRP Tuber Crops, Thiruvananthapuram
32. AICRP Palms, Kasaragod
33. AICRP Cashew, Puttur
34. AICRP Spices, Calicut
35. AICRP on Medicinal and Aromatic Plants including Betelvine, Anand
36. AICRP on Floriculture, New Delhi
37. AICRP in Micro Secondary & Pollutant Elements in Soils and Plants, Bhopal
38. lAICRP on Soil Test with Crop Response, Bhopal
39. AICRP on Long Term Fertilizer Experiments, Bhopal
40. AICRP on Salt Affected Soils & Use of Saline Water in Agriculture, Karnal
41. AICRP on Water Management Research, Bhubaneshwar
42. AICRP on Ground Water Utilisation, Bhubaneshwar
43. AICRP Dryland Agriculture, Hyderabad
44. AICRP on Agrometeorology, Hyderabad including Network on Impact adaptation & Vulnerability of Indian Agri. to Climate Change
45. AICRP Integrated Farming System Research, Modipuram including Network Organic Farming
46. AICRP Weed Control, Jabalpur
47. AICRP on Agroforestry, Jhansi
48. AICRP on Farm Implements & Machinery, Bhopal
49. All India Coordinated Research Project on Ergonomics and Safety in Agriculture
50. AICRP on Renewable Sources of Energy for Ag. and Agro Based Indus., Bhopal
51. AICRP on Utilization of Animal Energy (UAE), Bhopal
52. AICRP on Application of Plastic in Agriculture, Ludhiana
53. AICRP on PHT, Ludhiana
54. AICRP on Goat Improvement, Mathura
55. AICRP- Improvement of Feed Sources & Nutrient Utilisation for raising animal production, Bangalore
56. AICRP on Cattle Research, Meerut
57. AICRP on Poultry, Hyderabad
58. AICRP-Pig, Izzatnagar
59. AICRP Foot and Mouth Disease, Mukteshwar

60. AICRP ADMAS, Bangalore
61. AICRP on Home Science, Bhubaneshwar

Network Projects - 17

1. All India Coordinated Research Network on Underutilised Crops, New Delhi
2. All India Network Project on Tobacco, Rajahmundry
3. Network Project on White Grubs & Other Soil Arthropods, Durgapura
4. Network on Agricultural Acarology, Bangalore
5. Network on Economic Ornithology, Hyderabad
6. All India Network Project on Rodent Control, Jodhpur
7. All India Network Project on Jute and Allied Fibres, Barrackpore
8. Network project on Improvement of Onion & Garlic, Pune
9. Network Bio-fertilizers, Bhopal
10. Network Project on Harvest & Post Harvest and Value Addition to Natural Resins & Gums, Ranchi
11. Network project on Animal Genetic Resources, Karnal
12. Network Project on R&D Support for Process Upgradation of Indigenous Milk products for industrial application Karnal
13. Network Programme on Sheep Improvement, Avikanagar
14. Network Project on Buffaloes Improvement, Hisar
15. Network on Gastro Intestinal Parasitism, Izatnagar
16. Network on Haemorrhagic Septicaemia, Izatnagar
17. Network Programme Blue Tongue Disease, Izatnagar

Other Projects - 10

1. Technology Mission on Cotton (CICR, Nagpur)
2. Technology Mission on Jute (CRIJAF, Barrackpore)
3. Continuation, Strengthening and Establishment of Krishi Vigyan Kendras
4. Strengthening & Development of Higher Agricultural Education in India, New Delhi
5. Central Agricultutral University, Imphal
6. Strengthening and Modernization of ICAR Headquarters
7. Intellectual Property Management & Transfer/Commercialisation of Agricultural Technology (Upscaling of existing component IPR HQ)
8. Indo US Knowledge Initiative
9. National Agricultural Innovative Project, New Delhi
10. National Fund for Basic and Strategic Research, New Delhi

